The MEIT Revolution: Transforming Media Speculation into Institutional Yield through REIT-Style Structuring and STOs

The Media Entertainment Investment Trust (MEIT) Playbook

Author
Matthew Ashburn

The Assets & Data Playbook Series

The Media Entertainment Investment Trust (MEIT) Playbook

The MEIT Revolution: Transforming Media Speculation into Institutional Yield through REIT-Style Structuring and STOs

Matthew Ashburn

Matthew Ashburn

Published by Matthew Ashburn

Beverly Hills, California, USA.

website: https://matthewashburn.com/

Softcover ISBN: 979-8-9929021-8-1

E-book ISBN: 979-8-9929021-9-8

Book Cover: Matthew Ashburn

This book was created with assistance from Gemini AI, *a tool developed by Google.*

The author is responsible for all content.

1.2 Edition, Revised August 2026

Legal Disclaimer and Disclosure

1. General Information Only

The information provided in Private Datasets: The Architecture of Sovereign Issuance is for educational, informational, and illustrative purposes only. The concepts presented—including the Media Entertainment Investment Trust (MEIT), the D-MAFFO Equation and among other presented equations, and the Liquidity Stack—represent a theoretical framework for the institutional management of Media IP and Private Datasets. These models do not constitute a "get-rich-quick" scheme or a guarantee of future financial performance.

2. Not Financial or Investment Advice

Matthew Ashburn is a strategist and architect, not a licensed financial advisor, broker-dealer, or tax professional. Nothing in this book should be construed as financial, investment, legal, or tax advice. The purchase, sale, or securitization of Intellectual Property (IP), Private Datasets, and Digital Assets involves significant risk. Readers should consult with qualified professionals—including SEC-compliant legal counsel and licensed tax advisors—before implementing any strategies related to Security Token Offerings (STOs), private placements, or data sovereignty frameworks.

3. Regulatory Compliance

The discussion of Rule 144A, Regulation S, and Security Token Offerings refers to complex regulatory frameworks that vary significantly by jurisdiction. The author does not guarantee that any specific structure described herein will meet the current or future regulatory requirements of the U.S. Securities and Exchange Commission (SEC) or any other global regulatory body. Full regulatory compliance and the legal standing of any issued digital asset are the sole responsibility of the individual or entity implementing the model.

4. Accuracy of Data and Projections

While every effort has been made to ensure the accuracy of the financial modeling and "Shadow Value" concepts regarding Private Datasets and Media IP, the entertainment and data markets are inherently volatile. Case studies, "18-month capital cycles," and yield projections are hypothetical examples used for modular demonstration. Actual results will vary based on shifting market conditions, asset quality, and management execution.

5. No Fiduciary Relationship

COPYRIGHT

Contents

Disclaimer

This playbook is a structural exercise intended to demonstrate the mechanics of the MEIT framework, *D-MAFFO* framework and MEIT asset management. It is not a solicitation to buy or sell securities, nor does it constitute a formal offering memorandum. All figures and charts, including the $1B scaling simulation and dividend yield projections, are hypothetical models based on defined assumptions. Individual results will vary based on market conditions, asset selection, and regulatory changes. Seek independent legal and financial counsel before making any investment decisions.

Notice of Technical Status

Edition 1.2

This first edition of The Media Entertainment Investment Trust (MEIT) Playbook is presented as a foundational strategic framework and an invitation to the global financial and media communities. Please be advised that the methodologies contained herein—including the ***D-MAFFO*** Equation among others and the MEIT Structural Framework—have not yet undergone formal academic or institutional peer review as of this printing.

The author is committed to the continuous refinement and institutionalization of these concepts. As this framework is socialized among qualified institutional bankers, specialized legal counsel, and economic scholars, the author will release revised editions to incorporate peer-reviewed data, refined regulatory feedback, and updated industrial benchmarks. This work serves as the "Living Protocol" for the future of MEIT framework.

Forward

My journey in asset architecture is driven by a passion to transcend 20th-century constraints—honoring capital and craftsmanship while building enduring, institutional-grade wealth.

The Media Entertainment Investment Trust (MEIT) Playbook presents a groundbreaking blueprint for the modern studio. Inspired by REIT mechanics, the MEIT shifts entertainment finance from high-risk, single-title bets to plural, asset-backed portfolio structures—re-underwriting creative IP and private datasets as Digital Land and Buildings.

By uniting distribution revenue with high-margin AI data licensing, the MEIT potentially unlocks a scalable, yield-bearing asset class designed for enhanced liquidity. Institutional capital receives priority downside protections, while top talent gains long-term project backing and potential equity participation—aligning investors and creators in a perpetual, cash-flowing digital estate.

Executive Summary: THE MEIT PLAYBOOK

My journey in asset architecture has always been fueled by a deep passion for creating financial models that bridge the trappings of the 20th century to create anew—establishing modern means to honor capital and craftsmanship while building enduring, institutional-grade wealth. For decades, the fundamental flaw in entertainment finance has not been a lack of brilliant ideas, but an overreliance on fragile, single-project deal structures. Isolating investment into individual titles forces creators and investors to bear binary, all-or-nothing risk—a model that stifles innovation and leaves immense long-term value on the table.

The moment has arrived to pioneer a new financial framework. By shifting from isolated, single-title bets to plural, diversified portfolio structures, The Media Entertainment Investment Trust (MEIT) introduces a breakthrough in asset design. Inspired by the capital efficiency of Real Estate Investment Trusts, the MEIT establishes a scalable model that unites creative content and digital intelligence into a single, perpetual estate.

THE MEIT UNIFIED MEDIA ESTATE

ACTIVE SLATES: Pre-Money IP; Films, TV, Web Channels, Podcasts & Gaming

EVERGREEN IP: Post-Money Licensing and Residual Streams

PRIVATE DATASETS: AI & Tech Yield

Historically, as a film or series completed its theatrical or broadcast run, its primary distribution revenue naturally tapered off. But in the era of artificial intelligence and spatial computing, the secondary digital data generated during production—scene telemetry, 3D spatial scans, audio maps, and performance metadata—grows more valuable over time. Tech platforms urgently require ethically sourced, studio-grade datasets to train tomorrow's digital systems.

By uniting creative intellectual property and private data into a single, cross-collateralized estate, the MEIT unlocks three key breakthroughs:

Re-Underwriting Media IP and Private Datasets as a Unified Asset Class: Uniting decaying entertainment distribution revenue with persistent, high-margin AI data licensing streams compresses borrowing costs and expands credit limits, transforming unmonetized telemetry into a permanent balance-sheet engine.

Shifting from Single-to-Plural Deal Structures: Moving away from isolated, high-risk single-project bets and rigid private equity funds, the MEIT aggregates active slates, evergreen catalogs, and data vaults into a diversified, multi-channel portfolio that distributes risk and compounds yield continuously.

Distributed Equity and Liquidity Stack: Structuring a modernized capital stack where institutional capital receives preferred principal protection and hurdle priorities, while elite creators retain permanent, non-dilutable equity—transitioning artists from temporary fee-earners into lifelong co-owners of the estate.

At its core, the MEIT framework re-establishes media IP and private datasets as the modern equivalent of Digital Land and Buildings—a scalable, highly liquid, and yield-bearing asset class for the 21st century. Just as prime commercial real estate generates stable rent roll across changing economic cycles, a unified media estate produces recurring yield from both traditional viewership and continuous digital licensing. Every film slate, character franchise, and production dataset acts as permanent infrastructure, establishing an expansive digital footprint that appreciates in value as technology scales.

By uniting visionary storytellers, institutional capital, and technology platforms around this real-property model, the MEIT transforms creative content into a secure, sovereign store of value. We bridge physical production and computational utility, forging an institutional-grade investment vehicle designed to deliver long-term capital preservation, sustainable cash flow, and generational wealth.

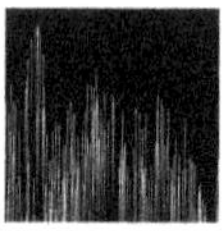

Chapter One

The Death of the Project, The Birth of the Portfolio

From its inception, the entertainment industry has functioned not as a stable infrastructure, but as a high-stakes casino. In the legacy framework, the **Project** is the fundamental unit of measure. This creates a structural environment where every film, series, or album is treated as a "*start-up*" that is birthed in debt and dissolved upon completion.

For the Executive Producer and the stake holders alike, this model enforces a Single-Asset Gamble. When 100% of the capital is tied to the performance of one title, success is binary: you are either a "**hit**" or a "**write-off**." *This is the definition of Systemic Fragility.*

The Three Fractures of the Project Model

The "Casino" model fails because it relies on three points of terminal instability:

Binary Risk (The All-or-Nothing Bet): In the project model, there is no "middle ground." If a $20M feature film fails to capture the cultural zeitgeist in its opening weekend, the capital is incinerated. There is no diversified safety net to catch the fall.

Accounting Opacity (The Black Box): Profits are frequently obscured behind project-specific "distribution fees" and "marketing overhead." In the legacy world, a project can be a global success on screen and a "net loss" on the balance sheet, leaving talent and secondary investors with "points" that have zero cash-flow value.

The Illiquidity Trap: Capital is trapped for 5–7 years waiting for a "waterfall" that may never flow. Investors are forced into a "buy and pray" posture, with no secondary market to exit their position if the project's internal rate of return (IRR) begins to decay.

The Innovation: Ending the "Lightning Strike" Era

The MEIT revolution begins by ending the *Project* and birthing the **Portfolio**. We stop treating media as a series of isolated creative events and start treating it as a Class of Productive Assets.

In a portfolio model, we don't bet on the "lightning strike" of *a single movie*; we own the Grid that captures the lightning. By rolling up hundreds of "Evergreen" titles—balanced with high-margin Private Datasets—into a single trust, we achieve Competitive Diversified Resilience.

The Portfolio Shield: Hedging Creative Volatility

The Birth of the Portfolio allows the Asset Manager to apply "Shield Logic." When you own a diversified collection of assets licensed across global territories, **a single "flop" is no longer a catastrophe**—it is a statistical outlier smoothed over by the recurring yield of the broader library.

Yield Management vs. Capital Gains: We move from "selling the asset to survive" to "owning the asset to thrive."

The Power of Evergreens: We use the stable, predictable cash flow of the past to fund the optimized, data-rich production of the future.

The Stake in the Ground

> The legacy industry chases the 'Hit.' The MEIT Asset Manager builds the Infrastructure. By shifting the unit of measure from the Project to the Portfolio, we remove the desperation from the creative process. We are no longer gamblers in a casino; we are Digital Landlords governing a high-velocity cash-flow properties.

The Illiquidity Trap: Why Capital Remains Frozen in Legacy "Waterfall" Accounting

In the legacy "**Singular**" model, the greatest enemy of the investor is not just the risk of a "flop"—*it is the velocity of capital*, or more accurately, the lack thereof. When capital is deployed into a single-project production, it enters a "black hole" of inefficiencies and illiquidity. Under traditional Hollywood accounting, that capital is effectively frozen for a period of 5 to 7 years, trapped behind a complex, non-transparent mechanism known as the Distribution Waterfall.

The Anatomy of the Freeze

In a standard project-based investment, your capital is subject to a chronological and contractual "wait-list" that prioritizes every entity except the primary risk-taker.

The Recoupment Queue: Before a single dollar of yield reaches the investor, the "Waterfall" must first satisfy:

Bank Debt & Completion Bonds: Senior lenders who take their cut plus interest.

Distribution Fees: Middlemen who take 15–35% off the top for "selling" the film.

P&A (Prints and Advertising): Massive marketing spends that must be recouped in full before "Net Profits" are even calculated.

The Time-Value Erosion: Because this process takes years to cycle through international territories and home entertainment windows, the Internal Rate of Return (IRR) of the investment is constantly being eroded by inflation and opportunity cost.

The Reality of the Trap: In the legacy world, a project can be a global cultural phenomenon on screen, yet remain a "fiscal loss" on paper for a decade. This creates a Desperation Discount, where talent and early investors are forced to sell their "points" for pennies on the dollar just to achieve a liquid exit.

The MEIT Solution: High-Velocity Liquidity via the 144A Rail

The MEIT Playbook solves the illiquidity trap by replacing the stagnant "*Project Waterfall*" with the Active Portfolio Stream.

From Years to Seconds: By wrapping the Media IP and Private Datasets into a BDC/RIC structure, we move the "exit" from a 7-year wait to *a 24/7 tradable event on the Rule 144A STO Rail*.

The Secondary Market Advantage: Qualified Institutional Buyers (QIBs) do not have to wait for a film's "home video window" to see a return. They can trade their position based on the Net Asset Value (NAV) of the entire portfolio at any time.

Real-Time Yield: Instead of waiting for a "Final Accounting" statement, token holders receive distributions based on the *D-MAFFO* of the entire grid, providing immediate cash velocity.

The Stake in the Ground

> Illiquidity is a tax on the creative class. The legacy 'Waterfall' is a relic of a pre-digital age designed to keep capital trapped in the hands of the gatekeepers. In the MEIT, we have engineered a vehicle where capital is as liquid as the data it generates. We don't just create value; we give it Velocity.

Owning the Grid: Transitioning from "Lightning Strike" Events to a Class of Productive Assets

In the legacy "Casino" model, the industry is addicted to the "Lightning Strike"—the singular, unpredictable blockbuster that justifies years of failed bets. This reliance on the "Hit" is not a business strategy; it is a binary event. It treats culture as a series of disconnected explosions rather than a steady flow of energy.

The MEIT Asset Management Playbook replaces the pursuit of the lightning bolt with the construction of the Grid. We shift the focus from the event to the infrastructure, transforming volatile creative labor into a Class of Productive Assets.

Building the Grid: The Infrastructure of Culture

Transitioning to the Portfolio means building a "**Cultural Power Grid**" that captures and distributes value regardless of which individual asset is currently "peaking."

The Unit of Measure: We stop counting "tickets sold" and start counting Asset Density.

The "Evergreen" Base Load: Just as a power grid relies on "base load" power (nuclear or hydro) to keep the lights on, the MEIT uses a foundation of Catalog IP and Evergreen Assets to provide a steady floor of **M-Yield**.

The Peak Demand: New productions act as "The Hits." When a project becomes a massive hit, it surges through the existing Grid, instantly increasing the valuation of the associated Private Datasets and cross-collateralized IP.

The Productive Asset Class: Beyond "Content"

By "**Owning the Grid**," the Asset Manager treats Media IP and Private Datasets as Productive Assets—entities that produce a measurable, recurring utility.

Lightning Strike versus The Grid

Attribute	The Lightning Strike (Legacy)	The Grid (MEIT Portfolio)
Nature	Discrete Event	Continuous Utility
Risk Profile	Speculative / Binary	Industrial / Diversified
Asset Behavior	Depreciating "Hit"	Compounding "Refinery"
Valuation Metric	Box Office / Streams	***D-MAFFO*** **/ NAV**

Harnessing the "Shadow Value"

The Grid allows us to capture what we call Shadow Value—*the data and metadata that usually evaporates after a project ends.* In the MEIT, every frame of film and every line of code is a "node" in the Grid. This infrastructure ensures that even if a specific story doesn't "strike lightning" with the public, its Private Dataset remains a productive asset that yields licensing revenue from AI partners, advertisers and global industrial partners.

The Stake in the Ground

We are moving from being meteorologists chasing storms to being engineers governing the utility. In the MEIT, we don't pray for the lightning; we own the Grid that makes the lightning profitable, predictable, and permanent. We have turned the 'Magic' of Hollywood into the Industrial Yield of a Media Entertainment Portfolio.

The Portfolio Shield: Using Diversified Resilience to Turn Creative "Flops" into Statistical Outliers

In the legacy "Project" model, a single creative failure—the "flop"—*is a terminal event*. For a production company, it means bankruptcy; for a talent, it means a "cooled" career; for the investor, it is a 100% loss of principal. **This is because the legacy structure lacks a Shield.**

The MEIT Playbook introduces the Portfolio Shield, a structural application of Modern Portfolio Theory to the creative arts. By aggregating non-correlated Media IP and Private Datasets, we transform the "flop" from a catastrophe into a manageable statistical outlier.

The Mechanics of the Shield

The Shield is built on the principle of Cross-Collateralized Resilience. When you own a "Grid" of 500+ assets across multiple genres, languages, and formats, the failure of one asset to meet its media projected **M-Yield** is "*absorbed*" by the over-performance or steady-state yield of the others.

Smoothing the Curve: In a single-project model, your revenue graph looks like a series of violent spikes and deep trenches. In the MEIT, the Portfolio Shield flattens these into a consistent, upward-sloping yield curve.

Non-Correlated Alpha: Because the MEIT includes Private Datasets (**D-Yield**), a downturn in the "Consumer Media" market is often offset by the rising demand for "Industrial AI Training Data." **The data shields the media, and the media feeds the data.**

Turning the "Flop" into an Outlier

In a traditional studio, a "flop" creates a hole in the balance sheet that stops new production. In the MEIT, we re-categorize the "flop" using industrial logic:

The Media Floor: Even if a film fails at the box office, it still generates Structural Metadata and Persona Signatures.

The Dataset Hedge: The "failed" project's Private Dataset remains a high-value asset for AI licensing. Machines do not care about "Rotten Tomatoes" scores; they care about the fidelity and uniqueness of the human-authored data.

Statistical Dilution: In a portfolio of 50 assets, a single underperformer only represents 2% of the total NAV. The

Shield ensures that no single creative "gamble" is to threaten the 90% Distribution Mandate to the token holders.

Yield Management vs. Desperation Selling

The Shield provides the Asset Manager with the "Luxury of Patience."

The Legacy Trap: When a project fails, the producer is often forced into a "*Fire Sale*" to cover debts.

The MEIT Advantage: The Shield allows the Trust to hold onto underperforming IP, wait for a market shift or a "cult classic" revival, and optimize the ***D-MAFFO*** over an 18-month cycle without the pressure of a binary "hit or bust" deadline.

The Stake in the Ground

> The Portfolio Shield is the end of creative anxiety. We have moved from a world where one bad weekend could destroy a decade of work, to a world where we use Diversified Resilience to protect our capital and our culture. In the MEIT, a 'flop' is just a data point—and in the Private Dataset business, even a bad movie is good dataset.

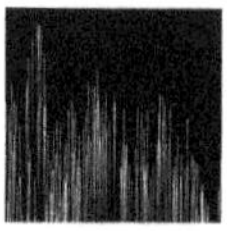

Chapter Two

The Digital IP and Data Landlord

To build a successful **MEIT**, *the Executive Team and business model must undergo a fundamental cognitive shift*: You are no longer in the "movie business"; **you are in the High-Margin Real Estate business**. The only difference is that your "land/buildings" are *constructed of pixels, performance, and code rather than brick, mortar, and steel.*

The Digital "Acreage": Scalability Without Limits

In physical real estate, a building's earning potential is capped by its physical footprint. To double your rent, you must build a second tower. In the MEIT model, IP and Datasets possess infinite scalability.

The REIT Parallel: A license deal with a global streamer or an AI lab is effectively a Triple Net Lease on a digital skyscraper.

The MEIT Advantage: Unlike an apartment complex, a digital asset can be "occupied" by 190 countries or 1,000 LLM training runs simultaneously, generating "rent" 24 hours a day with near-zero maintenance costs.

The "Evergreen" Anchor: Just as a REIT relies on "Class A" commercial leases, a MEIT relies on Evergreen IP. These are the "lo-fi" channels, classic sitcoms, classic films and educational series that provide the Institutional Floor, ensuring the 90% distribution mandate remains intact even during production delays.

The Institutional Leasing Engine: Anchor Tenants & Master Leases. We move from a "B2C" (Business-to-Consumer) mindset to a "B2B" (Business-to-Business) institutional leasing strategy. We no longer obsess over individual viewers; we focus on the Institutional IP Tenant.

The Anchor Tenant Strategy

In commercial real estate, an "Anchor Tenant" (*like Whole Foods*) provides guaranteed cash flow. **In a MEIT, global streamers (Netflix, Amazon) and AI Developers (Anthropic, Google) serve as your Anchor Tenants.**

Master Leases: We replace predatory distribution deals with Master Leases. We track the WALT (Weighted Average Lease Term)—a 36-month guaranteed revenue window that de-risks the portfolio.

Capacity Charges: We lease by the "Hour of Engagement" or "Token Generation," treating our IP and Data like warehouse square footage.

Ancillary Yield: While the Anchor Tenant pays the "Base Rent," the MEIT retains the "*Specialty Shops*"—TikTok clips, gaming rights, and merchandising—*driving additional high-margin revenue outside the lease.*

The Financial Engineering: The Heartbeat & The Shield

A Gold Standard MEIT replicates the rigor of Wall Street, utilizing a Three-Tier Legal Architecture:

The Master Trust (The MEIT): Regulated entity (BDC) managing global capital.

The Asset Management Company: The Executive Producer's firm curating the IP and Datasets.

The SPV Layer (Property Titles): Bankruptcy-remote "Property Compartments" for each individual asset.

The 18-Month Heartbeat

Fundraising is no longer a "*one-and-done*" frantic event. **We utilize a rhythmic, programmatic approach to capital:**

Months 1–6 (Acquisition): Deploying "Dry Powder" into distressed or under-managed IP/Datasets.

Months 7–12 (Optimization): Applying AI-localization and metadata enhancement to drive up the D-MAFFO.

Months 13–18 (Valuation): Marking-to-market and opening the next STO tranche at a higher token price.

Leverage & The DSCR Shield

We use Institutional Fuel (Revolving Credit Facilities) to fund production without starving the dividend. The DSCR (Debt Service Coverage Ratio) is our primary solvency test:

$$DSCR = \frac{D\text{-}MAFFO + \text{Interest Expense}}{\text{Total Debt Service}}$$

By maintaining a conservative LTV (Loan-to-Value) of 30–45%, the MEIT performs a "Yield Arbitrage"—borrowing at low institutional rates to fund high-return assets.

The Liquid Ledger: Fractionalization & Automated Governance

The **STO** (Security Token Offering) Engine changes the physics of media investment, breaking frozen equity into millions of digital "shards."

The Micro-Share: A $5M seed is divided into 5 million $1.00 tokens, allowing talent to be paid in precise equity bonuses (e.g., an producer receiving 5,000 tokens).

24/7 Global Liquidity: Tokens trade on regulated ATS (Alternative Trading Systems), allowing investors an "Exit-at-Will" without needing a total company buyout.

The Automated Waterfall: Smart contracts act as a programmable escrow. The moment a licensing fee (in Stablecoins) hits the Digital Treasury, the code executes an immediate split:

Maintenance Buffer (5–10%)

Asset Management Fee

90% Pass-Through (Pushed directly to token-holder wallets)

The Stake in the Ground

We are moving from the era of 'Pray for a Sale' to the era of 'Trade the Yield.' By adopting the Digital IP and Data Landlord mindset, the Executive Producer is no longer a freelancer chasing a 'big score'; they are an Asset Architect managing a permanent, scalable, and liquid financial utility. We have successfully turned the 'Speculation Trap' into a Diversified IP and Datasets Estate that pays the world while it sleeps.

Chapter Three

The MEIT (Media Entertainment Investment Trust)

To understand the **Media Entertainment Investment Trust (MEIT)**, one must stop looking at a film or a series as a "story" and begin seeing it as a High-Density Financial Instrument. *Structurally*, a MEIT is a specialized investment vehicle designed to aggregate, manage, and securitize a diversified portfolio of media assets and Private Datasets to produce consistent, passive income for its stakeholders.

It is the bridge between the high-growth potential of the entertainment industry and the disciplined, yield-centric world of Real Estate Finance. *The MEIT stands on three non-negotiable structural pillars:*

Pillar 1: The Pass-Through Mandate (The 90% Rule)

Like a REIT, the MEIT is designed as a tax-efficient "pass-through" entity under the BDC/RIC (Business Development Company / Regulated Investment Company) chassis.

The Mechanism: By distributing at least 90% of its Investment Company Taxable Income (ICTI) to token holders, the MEIT eliminates the double taxation typically found in corporate studio models.

The Goal: The Trust does not hoard cash; it flows it. This mandate ensures that the Yield—derived from both Media "Rent" and Data "Licensing"—hits the investors' wallets with industrial velocity.

Pillar 2: The STO Layer (The Security Token Offering)

Ownership in a MEIT is not represented by "shares" in a private company, but by Security Tokens issued on the Rule 144A (Private) or Reg A+ (Public) rails for example.

Asset-Backed Reality: Unlike "utility tokens" or NFTs, these are regulated securities backed by the actual Net Asset Value (NAV) of the IP library and the Private Datasets.

The Sovereign Ledger: Every token represents a legal, programmable claim on the $D\text{-}MAFFO$ cash flows. This layer provides 24/7 Liquidity, allowing Qualified Institutional Buyers (QIBs) to trade their position without waiting for a 7-year "Waterfall" exit.

Pillar 3: The Diversified Library (Media Entertainment IP + Private Datasets)

A MEIT never relies on a single "hit." Its strength is derived from its Biological Totality—the bundling of the "Land" (Media IP) and the "Infrastructure" (Private Datasets).

The Balanced Portfolio: The library must contain a mix of Evergreen Assets (reliable, recurring income), Active Tranches (new growth drivers), and Private Datasets (high-margin AI training fuel).

The Synergy: The Media IP provides the "Human Validation," while the Private Dataset provides the "Machine Utility." By owning both, the MEIT captures revenue at every touchpoint—from a fan watching a movie to an LLM learning a dialect.

The Stake in the Ground

> A MEIT is not a production company; it is an Industrial Utility for Culture. By codifying the creative process into these three pillars, we provide the one thing legacy Hollywood cannot: Stability. For the first time, a creator and a pension fund can coexist in the same capital stack, protected by a structure that prioritizes long-term yield over short-term speculation.

The BDC/RIC Formation: Step-by-Step Setup of the Business Development Company and Subchapter M Election

To transition from a speculative production house to an institutional-grade Media Landlord, the legal "chassis" must be precision-engineered. The MEIT utilizes a dual-layered regulatory structure: the **Business Development Company (BDC)** as the operational engine and the *Regulated Investment Company (RIC)* as the tax-efficient exhaust.

This is the "**Institutional On-Ramp**" that allows the Asset Manager to bypass the "*Desperation Discount*" and move directly into the 144A Private Rail.

The BDC Election (The Operational Shield)

The first step is incorporating a domestic entity and electing to be treated as a Business Development Company under the Investment Company Act of 1940.

The Proposed Filing: File a Form N-54A with the SEC. This officially notifies the commission that the entity is a BDC.

The 70% Asset Test: At least 70% of the MEIT's total assets must be "qualifying assets"—typically investments in private or thinly traded US companies (your IP-holding SPVs).

The Managerial Mandate: As a BDC, the MEIT is legally required to offer Significant Managerial Assistance to its portfolio companies (e.g., active "farming" of the Private Datasets).

The RIC Election (The Subchapter M Tax Pass-Through)

Once the BDC is established, the MEIT must elect to be treated as a **Regulated Investment Company (RIC)** under Subchapter M of the Internal Revenue Code.

The 90% Distribution Requirement: To maintain RIC status and eliminate corporate-level taxes, the MEIT must distribute at least 90% of its Investment Company Taxable Income (ICTI) to token holders annually.

Diversification Tests: The RIC must meet quarterly "asset diversification" tests to ensure the portfolio isn't overly concentrated in a single project, reinforcing the Portfolio Shield.

Creating the SPV Compartments (The Title Vault)

The MEIT does not hold the IP directly. Instead, it operates through a series of Special Purpose Vehicles (SPVs) to ensure bankruptcy remoteness and clean "Chain of Title."

Compartmentalization: Each 18-Month Tranche or major IP franchise is housed in its own SPV.

The Master Lease: The MEIT (The Trust) enters into a Master Lease Agreement with the SPV, governing the "Rent" (M-Yield) and "Data Extraction Rights" (D-Yield).

The Decentralized Ledger Integration (The Tokenization Layer)

With the legal chassis built, the equity and debt of the BDC are "wrapped" into a Security Token Offering (STO).

Smart Contract Logic: Hardcode the 90% Pass-Through Mandate directly into the token's distribution waterfall.

Compliance Coding: Embed Rule 144A transfer restrictions into the token metadata to ensure only Qualified Institutional Buyers (QIBs) can trade the asset during the private phase.

Audited NAV: Link the token's value to the Net Asset Value (NAV) of the bundled Media IP and Private Datasets.

The "Institutionalization" Checklist

Action	**Regulatory Body**	**Purpose**
Form N-54A Filing	SEC	To operate as a BDC.
Subchapter M Election	IRS	To achieve "Pass-Through" tax status.
SPV Formation	State Level	To isolate liabilities and protect "Title."
144A Private Placement	SEC / FINRA	To access institutional capital via the STO.

The Stake in the Ground

The BDC/RIC formation is the moment the 'Project' dies and the 'Asset' is born. By electing into this structure, we aren't just filing paperwork; we are Architecting Sovereignty. We have built a machine that is legally obligated to ignore 'Hollywood Accounting' and prioritize the 90% Flow of Yield to our token holders.

The 90% Rule: Engineering the Tax-Efficient Flow of Yield to Token Holders

The "90% Rule" is the structural heartbeat of the MEIT. It transforms the vehicle from a traditional corporate "structure" of capital into a high-velocity ***Pass-Through Engine***. Under the BDC/RIC (Regulated Investment Company) chassis, *the MEIT is legally mandated to distribute at least 90%* of its Investment Company Taxable Income (ICTI) to its stakeholders annually.

For the Token Holder, this is the end of "Phantom Profits" and the beginning of Industrial Yield.

Eliminating the "Corporate Tax Drag"

In the legacy studio model (C-Corp), profits are taxed twice: first at the corporate level (21%) and again at the individual level when dividends are paid. This "*Double Taxation*" erodes the actual value of the creative work before it ever reaches the participants.

The MEIT Innovation: Proposing by electing Subchapter M status, the MEIT is treated as a "transparent" entity for tax purposes. As long as the 90% distribution threshold is met, the Trust itself pays zero federal corporate income tax.

The Result: 100% of the earned yield from Media "Rent" and Data "Licensing" flows through the entity, ensuring that the Token Holder receives the maximum possible "Gross" return.

The Smart Contract Waterfall: Automating the Yield

To ensure "Truth" in the distribution, the 90% Rule is not left to human discretion; it is hardcoded into the Private Ledger. The yield flows through a three-stage mechanical filter:

The Inflow (Gross Receipts): All M-Yield (Streaming/Royalties) and GDI (Gross Data Inflow from AI licensing) are collected into the Trust's SPV compartments.

The Operational Filter: The Asset Manager deducts audited operating expenses and the DCAPEX required to keep the Private Datasets "fresh."

The 90% Trigger: The remaining Investment Company Taxable Income (ICTI) is automatically pushed to the verified wallets of Token Holders.

Yield Density: The Metric of the Digital Landlord

In the MEIT, we stop measuring "Profit Margins" and start measuring Yield Density per Token. * Priority of Distribution: Because the 90% Rule is a legal mandate, the Token Holders (including holding senior equity) are positioned at the front of the capital stack.

Non-Dilutive Growth: Since the Trust must distribute 90% of income, growth is funded by 18-Month Tranche Raises rather than withholding the Token Holders' yield. This ensures a constant, predictable "Rental" income for the investor.

Comparing the Payout Models

Feature	Legacy Studio (C-Corp)	MEIT (BDC/RIC)
Tax Treatment	Double Taxed (Corp + Personal)	**Single Taxed (Pass-Through)**
Payout Mandate	Discretionary (often 0)	**Legal Mandate (90% of ICTI)**
Accounting	"Hollywood Accounting" (Hidden)	**Audited / On-Chain (Transparent)**
Investor Status	Passive Speculator	**Yield-Bearing Token Holder**

The Stake in the Ground

The 90% Rule is the ultimate proof of Sovereignty. In a MEIT, we have engineered a system where the value of the art and the data cannot be trapped in a corporate black box. We have replaced the

'Promise' of a backend check with the Legal Obligation of a tax-efficient yield. We don't just create value; we ensure it hits the Token Holder's wallet.

The SPV Architecture: Protecting the Portfolio through Bankruptcy-Remote "Property" Compartments

In the legacy studio system, a single lawsuit or a failed production can contaminate an entire company's balance sheet. To build an institutional-grade Media Landlord model, we must adopt the structural rigor of commercial real estate. We do this through the Special Purpose Vehicle (SPV) Architecture, creating "*Legal Firewalls*" that turn every IP asset into a standalone, bankruptcy-remote property.

In the MEIT, we don't just "own" a movie; *we hold a Title (IP and dataset) to a specific digital estate within a protected compartment.*

The Concept of the "Legal Firewall"

An SPV is a subsidiary entity created for a specific, limited purpose—in this case, *holding the rights to a particular Media IP and its associated Private Dataset.*

Bankruptcy Remoteness: If one project (SPV A) fails or faces a legal dispute, the creditors of that project have no claim against the assets of the parent MEIT or any other project (SPV B, C, or D).

Asset Isolation: This structure ensures that the 90% Distribution Mandate remains uninterrupted. The "Grid" stays powered even if one "Transformer" (a specific IP asset) blows a fuse.

The "Property" Compartment: Bundling Land and Infrastructure

In the MEIT architecture, each SPV is treated as a **"City Block."** The Asset Manager ensures that the "*Land*" and the "*Skyscraper*" are legally inseparable within the compartment.

The Media Title (The Land): The copyrights, trademarks, and master recordings.

The Data Title (The Skyscraper): The Private Dataset, including persona signatures, behavioral metadata, and AI-training bibles.

The Master Lease: The MEIT (the parent Trust) enters into a Master Lease Agreement with the SPV. The SPV "leases" the rights back to the Trust in exchange for the capital required to "farm" and optimize the asset.

The Tranche-Based SPV Model

To maintain the 18-Month Tranche Cycle, SPVs are often grouped by vintage. This allows **Qualified Institutional Buyers (QIBs)** to see exactly which assets are backing their specific tranche of tokens.

The Seed SPV: Holds the foundational "Evergreen" assets that provide the base-load yield.

The Growth SPVs: Hold the active productions and newly extracted datasets from the current 18-month cycle.

Cross-Collateralization (The Portfolio Advantage): While the SPVs isolate liabilities, the MEIT structure allows for the yield to be pooled at the Trust level, providing the Portfolio Shield that protects the token holders.

Structural Comparison: Legacy vs. MEIT SPV

Asset Category	Legacy Classification	MEIT Classification
Catalog Films	"Library Content"	**Evergreen Land**
Raw Stems/Outtakes	"Production Waste"	**High-Density Infrastructure**
Audience Metadata	"Platform Property"	**Behavioral Telemetry**
Creator Persona	"Marketing Asset"	**Sovereign Signature**

The Stake in the Ground

In the MEIT, we have moved from the 'Handshake Deal' to the Architectural Fortress. By using SPVs to create bankruptcy-remote compartments, we treat our Media IP and Private Datasets with the same reverence a REIT treats a skyscraper. We don't just create culture; we Zone it, Protect it, and Insure its survival through structural engineering.

Chapter Four

The MEIT and STO High-Speed Rail

In the legacy entertainment world, raising capital is a fragmented process of chasing "angel" investors or navigating the opaque waters of studio and 3rd party financing. The MEIT bypasses this historical "Dirt Road" and moves directly onto the High-Speed Rail. This is the Rule 144A Private Placement—the institutional gold standard for securitizing high-density assets.

By issuing Security Tokens (STOs) on the 144A Rail, *the Asset Manager* connects the asset class directly to the deepest pools of global capital: the **Qualified Institutional Buyers (QIBs)**.

The 144A Architecture: Why the Private Rail?

Rule 144A is a safe harbor that allows the *Trust to sell unregistered securities to QIBs* (institutions managing at least $100M in assets). For the MEIT, this offers three critical advantages:

Speed of Execution: Unlike a public IPO, a 144A offering can be launched in weeks, matching the 18-Month Tranche production cycle.

Institutional Density: It filters for sophisticated "Strong Hands"—pension funds, family offices, and hedge funds—who understand the long-term yield of Media IP and Private Datasets.

Compliance by Design: The STO is not a "Crypto Token"; it is a digital security wrapped in the same legal protections as a corporate bond or a REIT share.

The QIB On-Ramp: Engineering the "Smart" Security

The 144A Rail is "Smart." Through the Private Ledger, we embed the legal restrictions of Rule 144A directly into the token's code.

Automated KYC/AML: The token will only transfer to wallets that have been verified as QIB-compliant.

The 90% Mandate Hardcode: The 144A investor doesn't have to "trust" the manager; the D-MAFFO flow is programmatically pushed to their verified institutional wallet.

The Secondary Market: While the rail is "private," the tokens can be traded among other QIBs immediately, providing 24/7 Liquidity that traditional private equity simply cannot match.

Pricing the Rail: The NAV vs. Speculation

On the 144A Rail, the token price is anchored to the Net Asset Value (NAV) of the bundled Media IP and Private Datasets. We move away from "Hype" and toward Asset-Backed Stability.

Feature	Traditional Film Equity	MEIT STO (144A Rail)
Investor Base	High-Net-Worth / Friends & Family	**QIBs (Institutions)**
Liquidity	5–10 Year Lockup	**Instant Peer-to-Peer (QIB)**
Valuation	"Box Office" Potential	**Audited D-MAFFO + NAV**
Issuance Rail	Private Contract	**Rule 144A Sovereign Ledger**

Stablecoin Integration: The Settlement Layer of the Rail

The 144A Rail utilizes a Stablecoin as the primary settlement layer to ensure frictionless value transfer.

Yield Settlement: When the 90% Distribution is triggered, the QIBs receive their yield directly in a Stablecoin, eliminating the volatility of traditional crypto markets and the delays of legacy wire transfers.

Capital Efficiency: By using a Stablecoin, the Trust can move capital between SPV compartments and global investors instantly, ensuring that the "Freshness" of the dataset is funded without the drag of banking intermediaries.

The Stake in the Ground

> The 144A Rail is the moment we stop playing 'Hollywood' and start playing Finance. By moving onto the Private Rail, we are telling the world that our Private Datasets and Media IP are not speculative bets—they are institutional-grade infrastructure. We have built the on-ramp; the QIBs are already waiting at the gate.

The Public Rail (Reg A+): Democratizing the Grid for the "Sovereign Community"

If Rule 144A is the engine of institutional capital, then Regulation A+ (**Reg A+**) is the "*Commuter Rail*" that opens the gates to the public. In the legacy model, "retail" investors are only invited to the party after the insiders have extracted the majority of the value. **The MEIT flips this script**, using the Public Rail to invite the Sovereign Community—the fans, creators, and small-scale yield seekers—into the same asset-backed ecosystem as the giants.

Democratizing the grid means moving from "audience members" to Grid Participants.

The Reg A+ Framework: The "Mini-IPO"

Reg A+ allows the Trust to raise up to $75M (Tier 2) in a *12-month period* from both accredited and non-accredited investors.

The Sovereign On-Ramp: This is a SEC-qualified offering that provides the transparency of a public company without the multi-million dollar "IPO Drag" of a S-1 filing.

Tiered Access: While the 144A Rail handles the massive industrial tranches, the Reg A+ Rail allows the community to buy into the Net Asset Value (NAV) of specific "Cult" or "Regional" portfolios.

Liquidity for the People: These tokens are designed to be traded on secondary Alternative Trading Systems (ATS), giving the community the ability to exit or increase their position 24/7.

The Sovereign Community: From Consumers to Co-Owners

On the Public Rail, the relationship between the creator and the audience is fundamentally restructured.

Direct Alignment: When a fan buys a token in a Horror Cult MEIT, they aren't just buying a ticket; they are buying a piece of the Media IP (The Land) and the Private Dataset (The Skyscraper).

Viral Distribution: Token holders become the most motivated marketing force in history. If the asset's D-MAFFO increases, their yield increases.

Governance Participation: While the Asset Manager maintains fiduciary control, the Public Rail allows for "Community Sentiment" polls to guide future 18-month tranches, ensuring the "Freshness" of the data matches current cultural demand.

The Stablecoin Payout: Frictionless Democracy

The Public Rail relies on Stablecoin distributions to solve the "*Small Check Problem*."

Micro-Yields: In legacy finance, sending a $5.00 royalty check costs more in postage and processing than the check is worth.

The Solution: On the Sovereign Ledger, a Stablecoin distribution costs fractions of a cent. Whether a community member owns 1 token or 1,000, their 90% Pass-Through is delivered instantly and autonomously.

Comparing the Rails Chart

Feature	The Private Rail (144A)	The Public Rail (Reg A+)
Target Participant	QIBs (Institutions)	**The Sovereign Community**
Capital Goal	Massive Scale / Industrial Floor	**Community Density / Liquidity**
Entry Barrier	$100M+ AUM	**Low Minimums ($100 - $1,000)**
Primary Value	Stability & Scale	**Engagement & Awareness**

The Stake in the Ground

The Public Rail is where the MEIT becomes a movement. By democratizing access through Reg A+, we are ending the era of 'Passive Consumption.' We are building a grid where the people who love the art are the same people who own the Data Infrastructure. The Sovereign Community doesn't just watch the show; they own the Yield.

Liquidity & NAV Floors: Protecting Stakeholders Through Audited, Asset-Backed Valuations

In the legacy "Project" model, a film's value is binary: it is either a "*hit*" or a "*write-off.*" This binary risk creates a liquidity desert for investors, *who are often locked into 7-to-10-year "waterfall" cycles* with no way to exit. **The MEIT** eliminates this structural trap by anchoring the STO Rail to a Net Asset Value (NAV) Floor.

By transitioning from speculative "*blue sky*" projections to audited, *asset-backed valuations*, we provide the Qualified Institutional Buyer (QIB) and the Investment Community with the two most important features of a modern security: **Downside Protection and Transparent Liquidity**.

The NAV Floor: The Industrial Safety Net

The NAV Floor is the total value of the "**Land**" (Media IP) and the "**Skyscraper**" (Private Datasets) divided by the total number of tokens in circulation. Unlike a stock price driven by market "hype," the MEIT floor is driven by the Replacement Cost and the Yield Potential of the underlying assets.

The Media Anchor: The value of the "Evergreen" library—its historical M-Yield performance—provides a baseline valuation that does not evaporate.

The Data Anchor: The Private Dataset is valued as an industrial commodity. If an AI firm is paying a GDI (Gross Data Inflow) to license the data, that contract acts as a direct "Floor" for the token’s value.

The PoHA Premium: We add a "Scarcity Multiplier" for *Proof of Human Authorship*, ensuring the floor is higher than any synthetic-only competitor.

The Audit Protocol: Third-Party Validation

To ensure the NAV is not a self-reported "hallucination," the MEIT undergoes a Quarterly Audit Protocol.

Independent Appraisal: A top-tier accounting or valuation firm assesses the fair market value of the IP and the Dataset licenses.

On-Chain Verification: The Sovereign Ledger displays the current ***D-MAFFO*** in real-time, allowing investors to verify the yield coverage of the NAV.

The Reserve Shield: A portion of the Stablecoin inflow is held in a "Liquidity Reserve" to facilitate orderly exits without crashing the token price.

Liquidity Without Dilution

In traditional finance, "Liquidity" usually comes from selling more shares (dilution). **In the MEIT**, liquidity is Structural.

The Secondary ATS: The tokens trade on Alternative Trading Systems (ATS) that are integrated with the 144A and Reg A+ rails. This allows for 24/7 peer-to-peer trading among verified participants.

The Stablecoin Buyback: If the token price ever dips below the audited NAV Floor, the Trust can use its excess

Stablecoin reserves to "buy back" tokens, retiring them and increasing the value for the remaining holders.

Valuation Comparison Chart

Metric	**Legacy Production Co.**	**MEIT STO Portfolio**
Asset Valuation	Intangible / "Goodwill"	**Audited NAV (IP + Data)**
Liquidity Event	Sale of Company / IPO	**24/7 Secondary Trading**
Downside Risk	100% Capital Loss (Total Flop)	**The NAV Floor (Asset Backed)**
Settlement	Legacy Bank (3–5 days)	**Stablecoin (Instant)**

The Stake in the Ground

> We have ended the era of 'Blind Faith' investing. In the MEIT, we protect our stakeholders by treating culture with the same fiduciary rigor as commercial real estate. By establishing an Audited NAV Floor, we ensure that even in a volatile market, our tokens have a structural value that cannot be ignored. We don't just offer a 'chance' at a hit; we offer a Seat on the High-Speed Rail of asset-backed growth.

Chapter Five

The Stakeholder Shift: Re-Engineering the Equity Pool

The traditional "Points" system in Hollywood is broken. Talent is often promised "Net Profits"—a mythical figure that rarely materializes after studio overhead, distribution fees, and interest are deducted. This creates a transactional, often adversarial relationship between the "creatives" and the "money."

The MEIT transforms this dynamic by Securitizing Human Capital. Instead of a promise of future profits from a single, isolated project, the MEIT offers A-list talent Security Tokens (STOs) that represent a fractional, liquid stake in the entire Equity Trust. We are moving from "*Work-for-Hire*" to "**Partner-in-Perpetuity.**"

The End of "Vaporware" Equity

In the legacy model, "Back-end" is illiquid. You cannot sell it, you cannot borrow against it, and you cannot verify it. A MEIT Security Token is a Hard Asset.

Direct Ownership: When a director receives 50,000 tokens as part of their "Signature Deal," those tokens are registered on the blockchain. They see them in their digital vault alongside their other institutional holdings.

Instant Verification: Talent can see the ***D-MAFFO*** flowing through the smart contract in real-time. The "Trust Gap" is closed by the transparency of the ledger.

Liquid Loyalty: The "Exit" Without the Sale

The most revolutionary aspect of the STO for talent is Liquidity.

The Secondary Market: Unlike "Producer Points," which are non-transferable, MEIT tokens can be traded on regulated Alternative Trading Systems (ATS) after the vesting period.

Financial Flexibility: If an actor needs to fund a new passion project or diversify their wealth, they can sell 10% of their tokens on the open market. They no longer have to wait 10 years for a "buyout" that may never come.

Cross-Portfolio Upside (The "Safety in Numbers" Play)

In the "Speculation Trap," if a director's movie flops, their equity is worth zero. In the MEIT, their tokens are backed by the entire library.

Diversified Risk: A director's tokens are supported by the yield of the "Evergreen" assets they didn't even work on.

Aligned Incentives: This turns the talent into a "Trust Ambassador." Because they own the whole MEIT, they are incentivized to promote all the Trust's projects, creating a collaborative "Studio Culture" that hasn't existed since the early days of United Artists.

Vesting for Value: Codifying Talent Retention

The Asset Manager uses the Smart Contract Governance layer to ensure long-term alignment.

Milestone Vesting: Tokens can be programmed to unlock based on specific performance goals: hitting a viewership threshold on a streamer, completing a trilogy, or staying with the Trust for 36 months.

The Golden Handcuffs: Because the tokens produce a 90% pass-through dividend, the talent receives a "Quarterly Royalty" for as long as they hold the asset. This creates a permanent income stream that replaces the "Residual" system with something far more lucrative and transparent.

Recruiting the Owner-Creator

By securitizing human capital, the MEIT wins the war for talent. We are not just offering a paycheck; we are offering a Capital Stack. A-list talent and EPs are increasingly looking for ways to build generational wealth that isn't dependent on the whims of a single studio executive.

The MEIT provides the "**Institutional Shield**" they need to turn their creative brilliance into a liquid, tradable, and appreciating financial asset.

Shifting away from "Hollywood Accounting": Using Blockchain Transparency as the Ultimate Innovation Recruitment Tool

For decades, "Hollywood Accounting" has been a dark industry joke—a system designed to ensure that even the highest-grossing films in history technically "**never make a profit**" on paper. This opacity has driven a wedge between the creators and the financiers.

The MEIT innovates "Hollywood Accounting" not through scaling, but through **Architecture**. By moving the entire financial lifecycle onto a public or permissioned blockchain, we replace "*Trust Me*" with "**Verify Me**." This transparency is our most powerful recruitment tool for the next generation of A-list creators who are tired of being "accounted" out of their success.

The Immutable Ledger: Real-Time Auditing

In the legacy system, *an audit is a multi-year*, multi-million dollar war. **In the MEIT, the audit is the Default State.**

Zero-Lag Reporting: Every time a licensing fee is paid via stablecoin or a "Master Lease" distribution is triggered, the transaction is etched into the blockchain.

Viewer-Side Verification: Talent can see the "inflow" from the streamers. There is no longer a "black box" where revenue disappears into studio overhead before the talent's share is calculated.

Eliminating Cross-Collateralization Abuse

Studios often use the losses of a failed "Project A" to wipe out the profits of a successful "Project B," effectively zeroing out the talent's backend.

Isolated Smart Contracts: While the MEIT uses the strength of the library to de-risk, the Smart Contract Waterfall for individual talent is "Hard-Coded."

Locked-In Splits: If an actor is owed 2% of the ***D-MAFFO*** from their specific project, that 2% is triggered automatically the moment revenue hits the wallet. It cannot be "offset" by an unrelated failure in another department unless explicitly agreed upon in the code.

The "No-Cheat" Administrative Layer

Legacy accounting relies on manual entries, "distribution fees" that can reach 35%, and creative interest charges on production loans.

Algorithmically Capped Fees: In a MEIT, management fees and operating expenses are capped by the Smart Contract Governance.

Smart Escrows: Instead of waiting for a check to be cut by a human accountant, the "Revenue-Share" is held in a digital escrow and released the millisecond the conditions are met.

Recruitment: Attracting the "Tech-Forward" A-List

The industry's top directors, writers, and stars are increasingly sophisticated about their "Business of One." They are looking for partners who treat them like Co-Owners, not vendors.

The Transparency Premium: Talent is willing to accept a smaller "Gross" percentage in a MEIT if they know that percentage is Guaranteed and Auditable, rather than a larger percentage of a "Net" that will never exist.

The Signal of Integrity: Being a "Blockchain-Native" Trust signals to the market that the Asset Manager has nothing to hide. This integrity becomes a competitive advantage, allowing the MEIT to out-negotiate traditional studios for the most coveted IP.

From Litigation to Cooperation

By ending Hollywood Accounting, the MEIT removes the primary source of friction in the entertainment industry. When talent knows exactly how much is being earned and exactly when they will be paid, they stop acting like "employees" and start acting like Strategic Partners.

The "Ledger" is not just a tool for the accountants; it is the foundation of a new creative era where success is shared, verified, and celebrated in real-time.

The Talent Magnet: Building a Creative Collective Where Everyone is an Equity Stakeholder

In the legacy studio system, talent is rented. In the MEIT, talent is invested. The traditional model creates a "mercenary" culture where actors and directors maximize their upfront fee because they know the "backend" is a mirage.

By contrast, **the MEIT functions as a Creative Collective**. Because the Trust is powered by liquid Security Tokens (STOs), every key contributor—*from the A-list lead to the visionary showrunner*—becomes a genuine equity stakeholder. This shifts the focus from "How much do I get paid today?" to "How much value can we build in the Trust together?"

The "Owner-Creator" Philosophy

The MEIT flips the script on labor relations. We treat talent as Co-Asset Managers of the IP they create.

The Equity Bonus: Instead of a traditional "performance bonus" paid in cash (which disappears), the MEIT issues Bonus Tokens based on critical or commercial milestones.

Long-Term Alignment: Since these tokens pay a quarterly dividend, the creator's wealth is tied to the long-term health of the library, not just a single opening weekend.

The "United Artists" 2.0 Effect

The original United Artists was founded by creators (Chaplin, Pickford, Fairbanks) to control their own destinies. The MEIT is the digital evolution of that dream, but with Institutional Liquidity.

Shared Prosperity: When one creator in the MEIT has a global hit, the NAV (Net Asset Value) of the entire Trust rises. This means the rising tide lifts all creators' boats.

Collective Power: A collective of 20 A-list creators owning a significant percentage of a $1B Trust has more negotiating leverage with streamers and tech giants than any individual agency or union could provide.

Democratizing the "Back-end" (Beyond the Top 1%)

Traditional profit participation is reserved for the top 1% of talent. The MEIT uses the efficiency of blockchain to push equity deeper into the creative stack.

Fractional Participation: The smart contract can effortlessly manage thousands of stakeholders. This allows the

MEIT to offer "Micro-Equity" to department heads (Cinematographers, Editors, VFX Supervisors) whose work is essential to the asset's longevity.

The Retention Moat: When the best VFX house in the world owns tokens in the MEIT, they are incentivized to provide their best work for every project in the portfolio, ensuring the entire library remains "Class A."

The "Creative Council": Governance as an Incentive

Equity isn't just about money; it's about Voice. Token-holding creators participate in the On-Chain Governance of the MEIT.

Strategic Input: Major stakeholders can vote on key Trust decisions, such as which new genres to expand into or which technological upgrades (like AI-localization) to prioritize.

The Magnetism of Respect: Talent gravitates toward the MEIT because it is the only institutional vehicle where their creative stature is matched by their corporate authority.

From Transactional to Transformational

The Talent Magnet strategy ensures that the MEIT is always the first choice for the world's most ambitious creators. By turning "Human Capital" into "Liquid Equity," we create a self-sustaining ecosystem of excellence.

When everyone is an owner, the "Speculation Trap" vanishes, replaced by a Diversified IP and Data powerhouse driven by the collective genius of its stakeholders.

Chapter Six

The MEIT Asset Management

The tragedy of the independent producer is their status as a "*Price-Taker*." When you approach a global streamer with a single film or a lone series, you are a supplicant. You lack the inventory to walk away from a bad deal, and the streamer knows it. They dictate the terms, the buyouts, and the "creative accounting."

The MEIT flips this power dynamic through Bundled Leverage. By aggregating a massive, diversified portfolio of high-performing IP and Private Datasets, the MEIT transitions into a "**Price-Maker**." At a certain scale, you are no longer selling a show; you are providing the essential Content Utility that the streamer needs to prevent subscriber churn.

The "Must-Have" Inventory Threshold

In the digital economy, streamers are terrified of Churn—the moment a subscriber cancels because they've "finished" the one show they came to see. A single hit attracts a subscriber, but a Library keeps them.

The Scale Play: When the MEIT controls 50, 100, or 500 titles across a specific vertical (e.g., "High-End True Crime" or "Gen-Z Animated Comedy"), it creates a Content Moat.

Systemic Importance: If the streamer loses the MEIT's entire bundle, they risk losing a significant percentage of their niche audience. This makes the MEIT's library "Systemically Important" to the platform's bottom line.

The Art of the "Master Portfolio Lease"

Instead of negotiating 50 individual contracts—which is a "funeral" for IP ownership—the MEIT Asset Manager negotiates a Master Portfolio Lease. This institutional-grade contract treats content exactly like prime real estate.

Key Provisions of the MEIT Master Lease:

Wholesale Arbitrage: The MEIT bundles high-margin "Evergreen" content with "High-Alpha" New Productions. The streamer gets a turnkey solution; the Trust gets a diversified ***D-MAFFO*** stream.

WALT (Weighted Average Lease Term): Fixed durations (e.g., 36 months) where 100% of rights revert to the Trust, growing the NAV.

Utilization Floor: If the streamer "hides" the content in the algorithm, the MEIT can trigger a "penalty rent" or clawback.

Data Mandate: The lease requires a real-time API Data Feed into the MEIT's dashboard. This transparency allows the Asset Manager to refine the ***D-MAFFO*** and prove the "Rent" should be higher in the next 18-Month Heartbeat.

Cross-Collateralization: The "Hit-Proof" Trust

In legacy Hollywood, a $100M flop craters a studio. The MEIT solves this through Institutional Cross-Collateralization, using the past to protect the future.

The Base-Load Protection: Before greenlighting a new production, the Manager calculates the "Surplus D-MAFFO" generated by the existing Evergreen library. This library acts as the "Base-Load" that covers the downside of new high-budget ventures.

The Performance Backstop: Within the Smart Contract Waterfall, a portion of the Manager's carry can be reallocated to satisfy investor returns if a specific release underperforms.

Hybrid Equity for Talent: We attract A-list creators by offering tokens that represent a claim on their specific project plus a fractional share of the overall Evergreen library. The talent is de-risked; the Trust is fortified.

The Content Loop: Killing Subscriber Churn

The MEIT replaces the linear "marketing funnel" with The Content Loop. By integrating high-frequency vertical content (TikTok, Reels, Shorts) directly into the lifecycle of feature-length IP, we transform "viewers" into "residents" of an ecosystem.

Breaking the "Ghost Town": We produce narrative-expanding "Satellite Assets" (Shorts) during the 24-month gap between seasons to keep the audience engaged 365 days a year.

Low-Cost R&D: We release "Micro-Pilots" in vertical format. If a character achieves viral velocity, we "up-level" that IP into a feature project, ensuring Accretion Protection.

Algorithmic Synergy: The MEIT owns its digital channels. We coordinate our social "Acreage" to create an external search spike, forcing the streamer's "black box" algorithm to promote our content to the "Top 10" rail.

Becoming the "Ecosystem Partner"

For a global streamer, the "One-Off Producer" is a liability. The MEIT, as an Ecosystem Partner, provides a solution to the streamer's most existential problem: **Subscriber Lifetime Value (LTV)**.

CAC Subsidy: By driving millions of organic viewers from our owned social channels to the streamer's platform, the MEIT effectively lowers the streamer's Customer Acquisition Cost.

The Data Bridge: Because we track engagement on our vertical social layers, we provide the streamer with "Early Warning" signals on trending themes, reducing the "Greenlight Risk" for both parties.

The Exit Option: The ultimate leverage is the ability to walk away. With our 18-month raise cycles providing cash reserves, the MEIT can credibly threaten to move the bundle to a rival streamer or launch a channel, or a niche DTC app if a streamer "low-balls" a renewal.

The Stake in the Ground

Bundled Leverage is the process of turning creative output into industrial power. When the MEIT reaches the $1 Billion Institutional Phase, it stops being a vendor and starts being a Partner-Competitor. By controlling the bundle and the algorithm, the MEIT ensures that the value created by human authors is captured by the Trust and its token holders, not just the platform's shareholders.

Chapter Seven

D-MAFFO: The Accounting of Media IP and Private Datasets

In the legacy entertainment world, *"Net Profit" is a phantom*—a shifting figure designed by studio accountants to vanish before it reaches the talent. In the MEIT, we replace this ambiguity with a rigorous, tax-governed baseline: **Investment Company Taxable Income (ICTI)**.

Because the MEIT operates as a *Business Development Company (BDC)* under Subchapter M, the "Truth" of our yield is not a creative choice; it is a federal filing requirement. ICTI is the bedrock upon which the entire MEIT Engine is built.

The Definition of ICTI in a Media Context

ICTI represents the net income of the Trust after allowable deductions but before the deduction for dividends paid to token holders. For the Asset Manager, this is the "Raw Fuel" of the distribution waterfall.

Revenue Inclusions: M-Yield: All gross licensing fees from streamers, theatrical rentals, and broadcast syndication.

GDI (Gross Data Inflow): Licensing fees from industrial AI firms for the use of the Private Datasets.

Interest & Dividends: Income earned from the cash reserves held within the SPV compartments.

Allowable Deductions: Operational overhead (the "Property Management" fee).

Interest payments on any leverage (debt) used to fund the 18-Month Tranche.

Audited production expenses.

Why ICTI Updates "Hollywood Accounting"

The power of ICTI lies in its Regulatory Rigor. Unlike "Contractual Net Profits," which are governed by private studio agreements, ICTI is governed by the Internal Revenue Code.

Standardized Rules: You cannot "hide" marketing costs in an ICTI calculation that haven't been legally expensed under RIC rules.

The 90% Mirror: Because the MEIT is legally required to distribute 90% of this specific number, the Token Holders have a direct, audited window into the actual performance of the "Grid."

The GAAP Alignment: ICTI must align with Generally Accepted Accounting Principles (GAAP), providing the transparency required for Qualified Institutional Buyers (QIBs) on the 144A Rail.

From ICTI to the Sovereign Flow

ICTI is the Audit Baseline, but it is only the beginning. While ICTI tells us what is taxable, it doesn't account for the unique "Maintenance" required for digital assets. To find the True Cash Flow—*the money available to grow the Trust and pay the people*—the Asset Manager must transition from the tax baseline (ICTI) to the functional reality: D-MAFFO.

ICTI = The Tax Transparency.

D-MAFFO = The Operating Transparency.

The Stake in the Ground

> We might have ended the era of the 'Accounting Mystery.' By using ICTI as our baseline, we have anchored the MEIT to a standard that even the most skeptical institutional investor respects. We don't ask our creators to trust our 'generosity'; we ask them to trust the Federal Tax Code. If the money is in the ICTI, it's on its way to your wallet.

The Rigorous Equation: Breaking Down the Components of D-MAFFO

If ICTI is the legal baseline, then D-MAFFO (Distributable Media Asset Adjusted Funds From Operations) is the functional heartbeat of the MEIT. In the world of **Real Estate Investment Trusts (REITs)**, "FFO" is the standard used to measure the cash flow generated by a property. In the MEIT, we have evolved this into a specialized industrial equation that accounts for the unique life cycle of Media IP and the high-margin utility of Private Datasets.

The *D-MAFFO* is how the Asset Manager proves to the 144A Rail that the yield is not just a "one-time hit," but a sustainable, compounding industrial flow.

The D-MAFFO Equation

The integration of Investment Company Taxable Income (ICTI) into the D-MAFFO equation is the essential link between regulatory tax compliance and institutional operational transparency. While ICTI serves as the audited "Net Income" for tax purposes, D-MAFFO serves as the "Cash-Flow Reality" for the investor.

In the MEIT framework, the equation is revised to use ICTI as the verified baseline, ensuring that the "*starting number*" is grounded in audited, industrial-grade reporting.

The *D-MAFFO* Equation:

$$\textit{D-MAFFO} = [\text{ICTI} + (\text{D\&A}) - (C_E)] \times (1 - \text{Delta } R_P)$$

Component Breakdown

ICTI (Investment Company Taxable Income): This is the audited net income of the Trust. It already accounts for gross revenues (RL + RD) and has subtracted operational expenses, management fees, and interest (OE + AM + ID). By starting with ICTI, the MEIT eliminates "creative accounting" and ensures the 90% distribution mandate is the floor.

D&A (Depreciation & Amortization): These are non-cash charges that reduce ICTI for tax purposes but do not leave the bank account. Adding these back reveals the actual liquid cash capacity of the library.

CE (Capital Expenditures): This represents the cash spent on recurring maintenance of the library (e.g., remastering, security updates for datasets) that may not be fully captured in the ICTI operating expenses.

1 – Delta RP (The Mechanical Adjustment): The multiplicative risk buffer that discounts the cash flow based on the portfolio's specific exposure to concentration risk, regulatory shifts, or technological decay.

The Relationship Hierarchy

Audited Compliance (ICTI): Proves that the Trust is operating within the legal bounds of a regulated investment vehicle.

Operational Velocity (*D-MAFFO*): Shows the "Real-Time" cash yield that the Media IP and Private Datasets are generating.

Risk Mitigation (Delta RP): Ensures that the yield is sustainable, protecting the "Institutional Estate" from the binary volatility of the legacy media markets.

The D-MAFFO Yield Ladder

The Asset Manager uses the equation to rank the assets within the Trust, ensuring the Diversification Mandate is met:

Tier	Asset Type	D-MAFFO Contribution	Goal
Tier 1	Evergreen Catalog	High ICTI / Low M-CAPEX	**The Floor (Yield)**
Tier 2	Private Datasets	High Margin / Low Maintenance	**The Alpha (Growth)**
Tier 3	Active Tranche	High D-CAPEX / Future ICTI	**The Refresh (Future)**

The Stake in the Ground

D-MAFFO is the math of the Sovereign Executive. It is the end of 'trust me' and the beginning of 'check the numbers.' By applying this rigorous equation, we turn the chaotic world of media into a transparent, industrial utility. We don't just hope for a profit; we engineer a Flow that is audited, predictable, and permanent.

The Data Alpha: Why Private Datasets Act as a Counter-Cyclical Hedge Against Traditional Media Volatility

In the legacy entertainment economy, when the consumer stops spending, the studio stops earning. Traditional Media IP is a pro-cyclical asset—it is highly sensitive to the "*Consumer Attention Economy*." If a recession hits or a streaming platform shifts its algorithm, the value of a film project can crater overnight.

The MEIT Asset Manager neutralizes this risk by utilizing the Data Alpha. ***By hard-coupling the Media IP with a Private Dataset***, we introduce a counter-cyclical hedge that thrives even when the consumer market is stagnant.

The Two Engines of the MEIT

The D-MAFFO equation is powered by two distinct revenue engines that operate on different economic cycles:

The Media Engine (M-Yield): Powered by Consumer Demand. It relies on "Hits," subscribers, and theatrical windows. It is emotional and volatile.

The Data Engine (GDI): Powered by Industrial Demand. It relies on AI developers, LLM training cycles, and synthetic media infrastructure. It is functional and persistent.

When consumer sentiment drops (Media Volatility), the demand for "**High-Fidelity Human Data**" often stays flat or increases, as tech firms use downturns to refine their automation models. This is the Data Alpha: the spread between the declining "*Attention Value*" and the rising "*Utility Value*."

The "Recession-Proof" Nature of the Vault

Traditional production is "Just-In-Time" (*you make a movie and hope it sells now*). The Private Dataset is "Just-In-Case" (you own the structural intelligence that the future is built upon).

Industrial Tenancy: While a consumer can cancel a Netflix subscription in one click, an AI firm signs multi-year Master Leases to access a specific Persona Signature or Linguistic Dataset.

The Scarcity Premium: In a market saturated with "Cheap" AI-generated content, the value of the MEIT's Fresh, Human-Authored Data actually increases. The Data Alpha turns the "Threat" of AI into the "Tenant" of the Trust.

Low Correlation: The correlation between "Box Office Performance" and "Data Training Utility" is near zero. A film that "flops" with audiences can still be a "top-tier" dataset for training emotional nuance in synthetic voices.

The D-MAFFO Rebalancing Act

The Asset Manager uses the Data Alpha to stabilize the 90% Distribution Mandate. If the M-Yield (Media) dips during an 18-month cycle, the Manager aggressively optimizes the GDI (Data) licensing to fill the gap.

Economic Climate	**Media IP (M-Yield)**	**Private Dataset (GDI)**	**Portfolio Impact**
Bull Market	High (Ad spend / Subs)	Steady (R&D)	**Maximum Yield**
Bear Market	Low (Belt-tightening)	High (Automation push)	**Stable Distribution**
Market Saturation	Low (Price wars)	High (Scarcity of Human Data)	**Hedged Alpha**

The Stake in the Ground

The Data Alpha is the 'Insurable Interest' of the creative class. By treating our work as a Private Dataset, we have built a shield that doesn't care if the 'Box Office' is up or down. We have moved from being victims of the 'Consumer Whim' to being the Industrial Suppliers of the most valuable resource on earth: Human Intelligence. In the MEIT, we don't just survive the downturn; we harvest it.

Chapter Eight

Velocity Economics in Media Entertainment Investment Trusts (MEITs)

Operationalizing 18-Month Tranche Architectures for Perpetual Asset Compounding

For institutional allocators and family office Chief Investment Officers, media and entertainment assets have historically presented a persistent portfolio paradox. While global demand for intellectual property (IP), evergreen content libraries, and entertainment consumption continues to expand, traditional private market structures fail to deliver optimal risk-adjusted returns.

Historically, institutional capital exposure to media has been restricted to two dominant vehicles:

Special Purpose Vehicles (SPVs): Single-project equity checks characterized by binary downside risk, high frictional cost of capital, opaque studio accounting, and complete lack of cross-collateralization.

Private Equity (PE) Rollups: Fixed 3-to-7-year closed-end funds that rely heavily on financial leverage, cost-cutting, and aggressive margin extraction to force asset liquidations prior to fund expiration.

Both models suffer from a fundamental structural flaw: they apply static, time-bound fund mechanics to *non-decaying, perpetual media assets.*

When capital is locked in a static 5-to-7-year PE lifecycle, the internal velocity of capital (V_C) drops significantly during development, production, and distribution lulls. This extended duration drag penalizes internal rates of return (IRR) and limits effective asset compounding.

The Media Entertainment Investment Trust (MEIT) framework resolves this structural inefficiency. By restructuring capital deployment into rolling, 18-month operational tranches, a MEIT transforms illiquid media allocations into a high-velocity, *multi-channel yield engine*. Principal capital is continuously recycled across active production slates, evergreen catalogs, and machine-readable data vaults, maximizing both short-term distribution yield and long-term capital preservation.

The MEIT Flywheel: How the Engine Gains Momentum

The core mechanism behind this high-velocity model is a continuous, self-reinforcing flywheel effect. Instead of starting from scratch with every new production, each 18-month cycle feeds the momentum of the next.

Here is how the flywheel builds compounding power:

Capital Fuels Craft: Blending patient private capital (such as family offices and institutional wealth) with strategic public funds (such as regional tax credits, cultural grants, and sovereign co-investment initiatives) provides non-dilutive leverage to finance active production slates led by top-tier creative talent.

Production Generates Dual Assets: Every shoot creates two valuable products at once: finished entertainment IP (movies/shows, podcasts, etc.) and high-density computational data (advertising content, 3D scans, scene telemetry, vocal maps).

Dual Streams Produce Dual Yields: The IP generates traditional distribution revenue, while the telemetry generates immediate, high-margin licensing fees from enterprise AI developers.

Yield Funds the Next Slate: High-margin data income pays out regular distributions to investors and creators while seamlessly replenishing the capital pool for the next 18-month production tranche.

Suggest that once this wheel starts spinning, the studio no longer relies solely on uncertain box-office hits to survive. The continuous baseline yield from AI data licensing, combined with the structural efficiency of blended public and private capital, keeps the flywheel turning—giving the studio competitive momentum and financial growth.

Theoretical Foundations of Velocity Economics

In institutional portfolio management, total return is governed not merely by gross profit margins, but by the frequency of capital rotation and the velocity at which liquidity is recycled.

Velocity Economics establishes that accelerating the reinvestment cycle of capital within a yield-bearing media estate yields a higher Effective Annual Yield (EAY) than relying on a terminal liquidation event at the end of a multi-year lockup.

The Capital Velocity Equation

Within a MEIT estate, Capital Velocity (V_c) is defined as the ratio of total annualized realized cash inflows—derived from primary distribution (R_{IP}) and secondary computational data licensing (R_{Data})—relative to the committed capital base (C_0) across an operational timeframe `T` :

$$V_c = \frac{\int_0^{\tau} [R_{IP}(t) + R_{Data}(t)]\, dt}{C_0 \cdot \tau}$$

Where:

C_0 = Initial capital commitment for operational tranche `k`.

`T` = Duration of the operational tranche (`T` = 1.5 years, or 18 months).

R_{IP} (t) = Primary distribution cash flows (theatrical, SVOD/AVOD licensing, international sales, syndication).

R_{Data} (t) = Secondary computational yield (scene telemetry, LiDAR spatial captures, vocal/performance maps, clean-room AI model training fees).

In a conventional 7-year private equity lockup (`T` = 7), delayed capital deployment and back-loaded revenue realization cause V_c to decay. In an 18-month MEIT tranche framework (`T` = 1.5), capital recycling initiates at Month 12, driving capital velocity significantly higher and mitigating internal cash drag.

Structural Architecture: The 18-Month Tranche Lifecycle

The 18-month tranche is engineered to align with the operational cycle of modern digital production, rapid global windowing, and immediate scene telemetry ingestion.

Lifecycle Phase	**Time Horizon**	**Operational Focus**	**Financial & Capital Mechanism**
Phase I: Deployment & Ingestion	Months 0 – 6	Development, principal photography, and real-time capture of raw spatial/scene telemetry (LiDAR scans, vocal maps, performance telemetry).	Capital deployed into production assets; telemetry ingested into bankruptcy-remote Sovereign Data Vaults.
Phase II: Primary Monetization	Months 6 – 12	Global theatrical/streaming premieres, initial licensing windows, and clean-room dataset structuring.	Influx of R_{IP} ; immediate realization of high-margin AI dataset ingestion and training fees R_{Data} .
Phase III: Liquidity & Recycling	Months 12 – 18	Secondary windowing, library catalog integration, and automated distribution/reinvestment calculations.	Recycled capital reallocated to Tranche k+1; preferred distribution yields paid to investors and creative equity partners.

By staggering and overlapping new 18-month tranches at 6-month intervals $T_1, T_2, T_3, \ldots$, the MEIT eliminates the binary release risk of legacy media slates. The estate generates a predictable, non-correlated stream of quarterly distributions for institutional investors while maintaining continuous capital deployment.

Mathematical Yield Dynamics: Compounding Return & Dual-Engine Revenue

To illustrate the mathematical superiority of an 18-month recycled capital structure over a standard static fund, consider an initial capital commitment C_0.

Effective Annual Yield EAY$) Comparison

For a standard closed-end private equity media fund generating a total investment multiple M over a rigid 6-year lockup period (`T` = 6):

$$EAY_{\text{Static}} = (1 + M)^{\frac{1}{6}} - 1$$

In the MEIT operational framework, a defined reinvestment fraction (alpha) of capital and realized yield from Tranche `k` is systematically rolled into Tranche `k`+1 at 1. 5-year intervals, while the remaining portion (1 - alpha) is distributed to capital partners:

$$EAY_{\text{MEIT}} = \left(\prod_{k=1}^{N} \left[1 + \frac{R_k - \text{OpEx}_k}{C_{k-1}} \right] \right)^{\frac{1}{1.5 \cdot N}} - 1$$

Where total tranche revenue $R_k = R_{IP,\,k} + R_{Data,\,k}$.

Because R_{Data} generates near-zero marginal cost cash flows starting in Month 6 through clean-room enterprise AI licensing, the numerator R_k scales faster than in traditional media finance. This early cash flow acceleration reduces portfolio cash drag and significantly expands the compounding envelope over time.

Non-Correlated Data Yield Acceleration

Traditional media revenue $R_{IP}(t)$ follows a standard decay curve characterized by high initial release performance followed by a trailing long-tail residual:

$$R_{IP}(t) = R_0 \cdot e^{-\lambda t}$$

Where λ is the natural distribution decay rate of the media property.

Conversely, secondary computational data yield $R_{Data}(t)$ exhibits inverse decay characteristics. As enterprise AI models, spatial computing platforms, and synthetic media engines require continuously updated, legally clean, and ethically sourced training datasets, the commercial value of studio-grade performance telemetry appreciates:

$$R_{Data}(t) = D_0 \cdot (1 + \beta t)^\gamma$$

Where β represents the computational data utilization rate and γ represents the model retraining frequency coefficient.

Combining decaying traditional media distribution cash flows with expanding computational data yield stabilizes total portfolio revenue, insulating the MEIT estate from macro economic cycles and box-office volatility.

Capital Stack Mechanics & Sovereign Governance

A core vulnerability of traditional media private equity is governance friction between financial sponsors and creative talent. Debt-laden PE rollups frequently impose aggressive operational restructuring, leading to talent flight and erosion of underlying IP value.

The MEIT framework introduces a Plural Equity Capital Stack that aligns patient capital with creative visionaries through structural governance rules:

Senior Preferred Structural Equity

- Investors, Family Offices & Institutional Asset Managers
- Priority return of principal C_0 + Baseline hurdle rate
- Senior claim on catalog cash flows and data revenues

Sovereign Common Creative Equity

- Elite Showrunners, Writers, Directors, and Actor Performers
- Non-dilutable equity share in production IP & Data Vaults
- Direct participation in secondary AI licensing yields

Risk Mitigation & Legal Insolvency Protection

1. **Bankruptcy-Remote Asset Isolation**: Production IP, evergreen libraries, and digital datasets are held inside independent Special Purpose Vehicles (SPVs) underlying the master trust, insulating investor capital from single-entity operational liabilities.
2. **Data Sovereignty Protocols**: Performer and creator telemetry (spatial scans, voice models, narrative metadata) is tokenized and governed via clean-room data vaults. Enterprise AI developers access datasets for training via secure compute environments without exporting raw proprietary files.
3. **Automated Tranche Auditing**: Capital distributions, residual calculations, and AI licensing royalties are calculated and verified at the conclusion of every 18-month tranche cycle, eliminating opaque legacy studio accounting overhead.

Strategic Implications for Institutional Portfolio Allocators

For institutional investors seeking yield, inflation defense, and non-correlated alternative exposure, the MEIT framework redefines media as a legitimate institutional asset class.

By integrating velocity economics and 18-month tranche architectures, asset managers achieve:

Shortened Duration Risk: Liquidity cycles accelerate from 7 years down to 18 months, reducing portfolio lockup risk.

Inflation-Hedged Cash Flows: Multi-channel licensing models (streaming, digital assets, spatial data, AI compute fees) provide multi-layered pricing power.

Structural Convexity: Downside protection is guaranteed by senior-preferred capital claims on evergreen catalog assets, while upside convexity is captured through exponential enterprise AI licensing expansion.

In an institutional environment where traditional static yield assets face compressed margins, the operationalization of velocity economics through Media

Entertainment Investment Trusts represents the next frontier in structured alternative asset management.

Chapter Nine

Institutional Strategy & Diversification

In the legacy "Project" model, diversity is often treated as a performative box to check. **In the MEIT**, diversity is an Institutional Strategy designed to maximize the Portfolio Shield. *By diversifying across regions*, formats, and genres, the Asset Manager ensures that the 90% Distribution Mandate is never reliant on a single cultural mood or platform algorithm.

We categorize our diversification into three distinct Operational Models (note; following is a small sample), each engineered to capture a specific type of Yield.

Model 1: The Regional Powerhouse

Capitalizing on the "Squid Game" Effect via Global Language Bundles

The "Squid Game" effect proved that high-fidelity storytelling can travel globally if the industrial infrastructure is in place. ***The Regional Powerhouse model focuses on Geographic Arbitrage.***

The Strategy: Invest in "Local-Language" IP (e.g., Tollywood, K-Drama, Spanish-language thrillers) where the production cost (MCAPEX) is lower than in Hollywood, but the Data Density is equal or higher.

The Global Bundle: We bundle these regional hits into a "Global Language Portfolio." This allows us to license the Private Dataset to AI firms training on specific dialects and cultural nuances, while simultaneously harvesting streaming "Rent" from a global audience.

The Yield: High-margin M-Yield due to lower production overhead, paired with high-value GDI from linguistic AI training.

Model 2: The Lifecycle Synergetic

Bridging Short-Form (YouTube/Social) with Long-Form (Feature/Gaming) Revenue

Traditional studios ignore short-form content as "marketing." To the MEIT Asset Manager, **short-form is the Top-of-Funnel Telemetry.**

The Strategy: Establish a "Lifecycle Bridge" where short-form assets (YouTube, TikTok, Podcasts) *act as a real-time R&D lab* for long-form IP (Features, Series, Gaming).

The Synergy: We use the behavioral data from millions of free views to "de-risk" the capital allocation for the 18-Month Tranche.

The Yield: The short-form provides steady, monthly M-Yield (AdSense/Sponsorships), while the long-form provides the "Lumpy" GDI injections from major platform licenses.

Model 3: The Global Cult

Dominating High-Loyalty Niche Genres (Horror/Sci-Fi/Anime) as a Specialized Brand

Mass-market "General Entertainment" is expensive and easily forgotten. **The Global Cult model focuses on** "Deep-Moat" genres with obsessed, recurring fanbases.

The Strategy: Specialize the Trust in a high-loyalty niche like Horror, Hard Sci-Fi, or Anime. These genres have a "Global Floor"—a base level of demand that exists regardless of the economy.

The Brand Equity: By dominating a niche, the MEIT becomes a "Vetted Brand." Fans will follow the Sovereign Signature across platforms, creating a permanent audience.

The Yield: High Net Asset Value (NAV) due to the brand's "Cult" status, and premium GDI from AI firms needing specialized genre-specific tropes and behavioral data.

The Diversification Matrix Chart

Model	Focus	Risk Profile	Primary Yield Driver
Regional Powerhouse	Language & Geography	Moderate	**Global Arbitrage /GDI**
Lifecycle Synergetic	Format & Funnel	Low	**AdSense / Data Telemetry**
The Global Cult	Genre & Loyalty	Very Low	**Brand Equity / NAV**

The Stake in the Ground

Diversity is not a moral goal; it is a Financial Fortress. By deploying these three models, the MEIT Asset Manager ensures that the 'Grid' is powered by multiple substations. Whether it's a Korean thriller, a YouTube documentary series, or a niche Sci-Fi cult classic, the Sovereign Flow remains uninterrupted. We don't just own one world; we own the Global Diversity of Human Attention.

The 18-Month Tranche: Mastering the Asset Management Cycle

The Industrial Cadence: Moving from "Project Fever" to "Capital Precision"

In the legacy model, production is a "one-off" fever dream. A film is finished when the money runs out or the director is satisfied—leading to budget bloat, missed market windows, and capital stagnation. The MEIT replaces this chaos with the 18-Month Tranche. This is the industrial heartbeat of the Trust: a fixed, repeatable management cycle that ensures capital is deployed, assets are refined, and Private Datasets are harvested with the reliability of a high-yield utility.

The 18-Month Tranche is the ultimate Asset Management Governor. It ensures the 90% Distribution Mandate is met not by luck, but by mechanical design.

The Anatomy of the Management Cycle

The 18-month cycle is divided into three distinct six-month "Value Stages." Each stage has a specific fiduciary objective designed to maximize the Net Asset Value (NAV) of the portfolio.

Stage 1: Capital Allocation & "Land" Assembly (Months 1–6)

The Deployment: The Asset Manager moves capital from the 144A Rail into specific diversification models (Regional, Lifecycle, or Cult).

The De-Risking: Using short-form telemetry, we finalize the "Blueprints" for the long-form assets. We don't green-light based on "gut feeling"; we allocate based on Audience Data.

The Goal: To transition from "Liquid Cash" to "Work-in-Progress (WIP)" assets as efficiently as possible.

Stage 2: The High-Fidelity Refinement (Months 7–12)

The Human Input: This is the period of creative "Drilling." We capture the performances, the bibles, and the raw stems.

The Data Extraction: Simultaneously with production, the Data Architect begins tagging the metadata and isolating Persona Signatures.

The Goal: To generate the highest-density "Physical Land" (Media) and "Digital Infrastructure" (Data) for the vault.

Stage 3: The Yield Event & Portfolio Refresh (Months 13–18)

The Monetization: The Media IP is "Leased" to platforms (M-Yield).

The Industrial Licensing: The newly "Fresh" Private Dataset is licensed to AI tenants GDI.

The Audit: The resulting D-MAFFO is calculated and prepared for the 90% payout.

Cascading Tranches: Ensuring Continuous Flow

To prevent "dry periods" in the yield, the Asset Manager utilizes Cascading Tranches. While **Tranche A** is in the "Yield Event" phase, **Tranche B** is in "Refinement," and **Tranche C** is in "Allocation."

The Overlap: This ensures a constant stream of income for the Token Holders.

The Compounding Effect: Each new tranche uses the "Infrastructure" (the Private Dataset) built by the previous one, lowering the MCAPEX and increasing the overall NAV.

The Tranche Performance Audit

At the end of every 18-month cycle, the Asset Manager performs a Fiduciary Review to determine the allocation for the next cycle.

Management Metric	**Target**	**Purpose**
Asset Density	>95% Utilization	Ensure no "Shadow Value" was left unharvested.
Freshness Score	1.0 (New Human Data)	Maintain the "Clean Data" premium for AI licensing.
Yield Velocity	***D-MAFFO* Principal Recovery**	To ensure the current tranche pays back its initial capital outlay within the 18-month window.
Token Pricing	**Floor Price Stabilization**	To provide a transparent, NAV-backed valuation for the **MEIT** issuance on the 144A Rail.
NAV Growth	+15% per cycle	Ensure the Trust appreciates over time through "Fresh" data compounding.

The Stake in the Ground

The 18-Month Tranche is the end of the 'Hollywood Wait.' We have turned the erratic timeline of the artist into the Industrial Cadence of the Executive. By mastering this management cycle, we ensure that our capital is always working, our datasets are always fresh, and our Token Holders are always paid. We don't just make movies; we operate a Cultural High-Rise that never has a vacancy.

Chapter Ten

The Securitization Roadmap

Phase 1: Aggregation: Pooling "Evergreen" Titles and "Shadow Value" Assets into the Trust

The transition from a collection of projects to a multi-billion dollar Information REIT begins with Aggregation. In this phase, the Asset Manager acts as a "Digital Land Assembler," identifying and acquiring the undervalued "Acreage" (Media IP) and the "Mineral Rights" (Private Datasets) that will form the collateral for the Diversified IP and Data Estate.

Aggregation is not merely a collection of files; it is the industrial process of moving disparate creative equity into a unified, high-security Private Dataset Vault.

The "Evergreen" Anchor: Base-Load Yield

The foundation of the Trust is built on Evergreen Assets. These are titles with proven historical performance and long-tail cultural relevance.

The Selection Criteria: We look for "Low-Beta" assets—content that produces steady, predictable M-Yield (streaming residuals and licensing) regardless of current market trends.

The Role: Evergreens provide the "Base-Load" power for the Portfolio. They ensure that the 90% Distribution Mandate is met from day one, even before the newer, high-growth tranches are fully refined.

Harvesting "Shadow Value": The Hidden Infrastructure

In the legacy model, "Shadow Value" is treated as waste. It includes the bibles, the outtakes, the raw stems, and the behavioral metadata generated during a production. **In the MEIT**, this is the High-Density Infrastructure of the Private Dataset.

The Extraction Process: We aggregate the "Master Stems" (isolated dialogue, music, and SFX) and "Persona Signatures."

The Valuation Shift: While a legacy studio might value a dormant 1990s sitcom at near-zero, the MEIT Asset Manager values it as a Premium Linguistic Dataset for AI localization models. Aggregation turns "Scrap" into Senior Collateral.

The Onboarding Protocol: Moving Equity into the Vault

Aggregation requires a legal and technical "Handshake" between the original creators and the Trust. This is the Aggregation Event:

The Title Audit: A rigorous "Chain of Title" review to ensure the SPV has exclusive rights to both the Media and the Data.

The Talent Conversion: Existing "Profit Participation" points are converted into Security Tokens (STOs). The creator moves from being an unsecured creditor of a studio to a senior equity holder in the MEIT.

The Vaulting: The digital masters and raw datasets are moved into a Zero-Trust Security environment. Once vaulted, the asset is officially "Zoned" for institutional licensing.

The Aggregation Matrix Chart

Asset Category	Legacy Classification	MEIT Classification
Catalog Films	"Library Content"	**Evergreen Land**
Raw Stems/Outtakes	"Production Waste"	**High-Density Infrastructure**
Audience Metadata	"Platform Property"	**Behavioral Telemetry**
Creator Persona	"Marketing Asset"	**Sovereign Signature**

The Stake in the Ground

Aggregation is the act of claiming our Information Sovereignty. We are taking the fragmented pieces of our creative history and pooling them into a single, unbreakable Trust. By bundling the 'Evergreen' land with the 'Shadow' infrastructure, we have created an asset class that is too dense to be ignored by the institutional rails. We aren't just collecting movies, shows, channels, etc.; we are Assembling the Grid.

Phase 2: Bundling: Hard-Coupling Media IP (The Land) with Private Datasets (The Skyscraper)

In the legacy world, a film and its production data are often separated—the film is sold to a distributor, while the raw data sits on a hard drive in a basement until it degrades. In the MEIT Asset Management Playbook, this separation is a catastrophic loss of value.

Bundling is the industrial process of "*Hard-Coupling*" the Media IP with the Private Dataset. By legally and technically fusing the "**Land**" (the creative story) with the "**Skyscraper**" (the high-density data infrastructure), we create a unified asset that is greater than the sum of its parts.

The Physicality of the Bundle

The Asset Manager does not view a "Bundle" as a folder of files. It is a Composite Security. To achieve institutional-grade valuation on the 144A Rail, *the bundle must be integrated at the architectural level*:

The Narrative Foundation (The Land): This is the "Surface Rights." It includes the finished film, the characters, and the brand equity. It is what the human audience "walks on."

The Structural Stems (The Skyscraper): This is the "Vertical Density." It includes isolated dialogue tracks, character behavioral bibles, motion-capture data, and linguistic nuances. It is what the AI "lives in."

The Hard-Coupling Mechanism

Hard-coupling is achieved through the Smart Asset Wrapper. This ensures that the two cannot be sold or licensed separately without the Trust's consent, *protecting the NAV (Net Asset Value) from dilution*.

Metadata Synchronization: Every frame of the Media IP is "Time-Stamped" and linked to its corresponding data stem in the Private Dataset.

Cross-Platform Licensing: When a streamer "leases" the film (Media), the contract includes a "Machine-Usage Restricted" clause. The "Machine Rights" (Data) are reserved for separate high-margin industrial leases.

The Valuation Multiplier: By bundling, the Asset Manager proves to investors that the "Land" is not just for farming (streaming); it is zoned for "High-Rise Development" (AI training).

Why the Bundle Wins: The "Industrial Anchor"

The bundle provides a Floor and a Ceiling for the investment:

The Media Floor: If the AI market is volatile, the "Land" (Media IP) still produces steady M-Yield from human viewers.

The Data Ceiling: If the entertainment market is saturated, the "Skyscraper" (Private Dataset) provides high-alpha growth through industrial AI licensing.

Feature	Raw Media (Legacy)	The Bundled Asset (MEIT)
Asset Type	Consumer Product	**Industrial Utility**
Revenue Stream	Single (Licensing)	**Dual (M-Yield + GDI)**
Durability	Subject to "Trends"	**Structural Utility**
Collateral Value	Speculative	**Senior Secured**

The "Zoning" Audit

Before the Bundle can be securitized, the Asset Manager performs a Zoning Audit. This confirms that the Private

Dataset is "Clean"—*meaning it is 100% human-authored and legally cleared for machine learning.*

Human-Authored Premium: We certify that the "Skyscraper" was built by human architects (creators), not machines.

Industrial Readiness: We ensure the data stems are formatted for immediate ingestion by Large Language Models (LLMs) and Synthetic Media engines.

The Stake in the Ground

> A skyscraper without land is a hallucination; land without a skyscraper is a waste of space. In the MEIT, we refuse to leave value on the table. By Hard-Coupling the Media IP with the Private Dataset, we have created the first High-Density Digital Estate. We aren't just selling a story; we are leasing the Foundation and the Infrastructure of Intelligence.

Phase 3: Validation: Auditing the Cash-Flow Engine Before Launching the STO Rail

Before a MEIT can transition from a private collection to a securitized asset on the Rule 144A (Private) or Reg A+ (Public) rails, it must pass through the Validation Phase. In the legacy world, "validation" *is often a subjective guess based on box office projections*. In the MEIT, validation is an industrial audit of the Cash-Flow Engine.

We do not ask the market to "believe" in the creative vision; we provide a transparent, audited proof of the ***D-MAFFO*** and the Net Asset Value (NAV).

The "Truth" Audit: Beyond Hollywood Accounting

Validation begins by stripping away the "Phantom Profits" of legacy accounting. The Asset Manager employs third-party auditors to verify the Investment Company Taxable Income (ICTI).

The Revenue Verification: Auditing the actual "Rent" collected from streamers, theatrical distributors, and music platforms (M-Yield).

The Data Inflow (GDI): Verifying the signed Master Leases with AI industrial partners and tech tenants who are licensing the Private Datasets.

The 90% Flow-Test: Proving that the vehicle's "plumbing" is legally and technically capable of passing 90% of this income directly to the Token Holders without corporate leakage.

Stress-Testing the Portfolio Shield

The Validation Phase includes a "Sensitivity Analysis" to prove the resilience of the Portfolio. We simulate market downturns to ensure the 90% Distribution Mandate remains intact.

The "Flop" Simulation: What happens to the yield if the next three 18-month tranches underperform by 40%?

The Data Hedge Test: Does the rising value of the Private Dataset offset a stagnation in consumer streaming subscriptions?

NAV Integrity: Confirming that the Senior Collateral (the hard-coupled Media/Data bundle) maintains a floor value that protects the principal of the Qualified Institutional Buyers (QIBs).

The D-MAFFO Certification

The ultimate output of Phase 3 is the Certified ***D-MAFFO*** Statement. This is the document that institutional investors on the 144A Rail use to price the offering.

Section	Component	Description
I. Baseline	**ICTI Verified**	The audited **Investment Company Taxable Income**; the tax-compliant floor.
II. Adjustments	**(D&A) Add-Back**	Non-cash Depreciation and Amortization restored to the liquid cash total.
III. Maintenance	**(Ce) Cap-Ex**	Deductions for essential library upkeep and dataset security refreshes.
IV. The Buffer	**Delta R_p Applied**	The multiplicative **Delta Risk Premium** coefficient (e.g., 0.90 for a 10% risk buffer).
V. The Output	**Certified Yield**	The final, risk-adjusted **D-MAFFO** figure used for 144A secondary market pricing.

The Pre-Flight Checklist for the STO Rail

Validation Milestone	Requirement	Purpose
Clean Chain of Title	100% legal clearance of all IP/Data.	To ensure the STO is "Asset-Backed."
PoHA Audit	Proof of Human Authorship for all datasets.	To command the "Clean Data" premium.
Smart Contract Audit	Cybersecurity review of the distribution code.	To guarantee the 90% Pass-Through.
Regulatory Filing	Form N-54A (BDC) & Subchapter M (RIC).	To finalize the tax-efficient chassis.

The Stake in the Ground

Validation is where the 'Art' becomes an 'Asset.' We aren't launching on a whim or a 'good feeling' about a script. We are launching on Audited Truth. By the time a MEIT hits the 144A Rail, the uncertainty of the 'Casino' has been replaced by the Predictability of the Utility. We have validated the engine; now, we open the throttle.

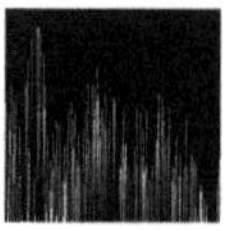

Chapter Eleven

Re-Underwriting Media IP and Private Datasets as a Unified Asset Class

This research paper outlines a financial strategy for commercial and investment banking institutions: the systematic refinancing of media and technology client portfolios by re-underwriting intellectual property (IP) copyrights and proprietary behavioral datasets as a single, unified asset class. Legacy credit markets and private equity (PE) sponsors consistently under-collateralize media enterprises by valuing media distribution rights separately from scene telemetry, user engagement metrics, and generative AI training data.

By unifying IP and Private Datasets into a consolidated collateral base, financial institutions can compress Weighted Average Cost of Capital (WACC), expand Loan-to-Value (LTV) limits, and execute large-scale portfolio refinancing across their broader clientele. This paper examines the mathematical valuation engine of unified asset underwriting, analyzes the structural shortcomings of traditional private equity and

Special Purpose Vehicle (SPV) models, and introduces the Media Entertainment Investment Trust (MEIT) framework as the optimal vehicle for long-term capital efficiency and market capitalization expansion.

Introduction: The Intangible Capital Mispricing Deficit

Intangible assets comprise over 88% of the market capitalization of modern enterprise indices, with intellectual property-backed lending exceeding $50 billion globally. Despite this scale, institutional debt underwriting methodologies remain anchored to legacy accounting standards that bifurcate content rights (e.g., film libraries, television catalogs, music publishing) from contextual execution data (e.g., spatial telemetry, interaction logs, generative model inputs).

Legacy Siloed Model (Bifurcated Capital):

- Media IP Copyrights (Valued on Linear Cash) —> *Discounted Debt Underwriting*
- Private Datasets (Unmonetized/Off-Bal) —> *Neglected Capital Capacity*

Unified Synthetic Asset Model (Integrated Capital):

- Cross-Collateralized Real-Time Yield Mechanics —> *Optimized Refinancing & Market Cap Expansion*

When media IP and data assets are siloed:

1. Media IP is appraised strictly on historical cash flow decay curves (e.g., traditional syndication and streaming licensing windows).

2. Private Datasets remain uncapitalized off-balance-sheet items or are lumped into unquantifiable enterprise goodwill.

This bifurcation creates a valuation discount. When an institution re-underwrites these assets as a single, interdependent entity, the primary creative content acts as the continuous origin engine for high-margin data telemetry, while the data telemetry provides perpetual secondary yield through clean-room AI model licensing and predictive analytics.

Structural Limitations of Legacy Capital Frameworks

Private Equity Exit Horizon Misalignment

Private Equity sponsors operating under traditional closed-end funds face a structural mismatch when holding IP and dataset portfolios:

- PE Horizon in 3, 7 years << IP & Dataset Economic Life in 50, 100+ years

Because PE funds are governed by internal rate of return (IRR) deadlines and forced liquidation dates, sponsors routinely strip cost centers, underinvest in long-term data collection infrastructure, and force premature asset sales. This cuts off compounding residual yields precisely as cross-licensing and machine-learning utility mature.

Debt Fragmenting and SPV Inefficiencies

Traditional media financing relies on isolated Special Purpose Vehicles (SPVs) for individual productions or single slates.

- High Transaction Costs: Legal, underwriting, and administrative overhead recurs per project.
- Non-Cross-Collateralized Risk: A failure in SPV alpha cannot be offset by outsized yield in SPV beta, forcing higher debt risk premiums.
- Data Leakage: Data generated within an SPV rarely accrues to the parent entity's balance sheet, depriving the borrower of long-term capital expansion.

Valuation Mechanics of the Unified Synthetic Asset

To establish an institutional credit framework for refinancing, financial institutions must model media IP and its associated dataset as a dynamic, coupled asset system.

Valuation Model Equations

Let $C_{IP}(t)$ represent the net operational cash flows from media distribution and licensing at time t, and let $C_{Data}(t)$ represent secondary cash flows generated through dataset licensing, spatial metadata, and AI training compute access.

The conventional valuation approach evaluates assets independently:

$$V_{\text{Siloed}} = \int_0^{T_1} C_{\text{IP}}(t)e^{-r_{\text{IP}}t}\,dt + \int_0^{T_2} C_{\text{Data}}(t)e^{-r_{\text{Data}}t}\,dt$$

Under the Unified Asset Model, cash flows interact synergistically through a positive feedback factor Omega(t), where engagement with media IP enriches the dataset, and dataset utilization optimizes content monetization and direct AI model integration:

$$V_{\text{Unified}} = \int_0^{\infty} \left[C_{\text{IP}}(t) + C_{\text{Data}}(t) + \Omega(t)\right] e^{-r_{\text{Unified}}t}\,dt$$

Where:

- $\Omega(t) = \alpha \cdot (C_{\text{IP}}(t) \times C_{\text{Data}}(t))^{\gamma}$ captures the cross-network economic multiplier ($\alpha > 0, \gamma \geq 0.5$).
- $r_{\text{Unified}} < \min(r_{\text{IP}}, r_{\text{Data}})$ due to risk diversification and reduced volatility across combined cash flow streams.

Discount Rate Compression and LTV Expansion

Cross-collateralizing media IP with active private datasets alters borrower credit profiles:

$$\text{WACC}_{\text{Unified}} = w_d \cdot r_d \cdot (1 - \tau) + w_e \cdot r_e - \Delta_{\text{Diversification}}$$

Where $\Delta_{\text{Diversification}}$ represents the reduction in beta achieved by offsetting cyclic media box-office/streaming variance with persistent, non-correlated AI dataset subscriptions.

Consequently, banking institutions proposing could safely increase standard Loan-to-Value (LTV) limits from legacy thresholds (25% - 35%) up to 45% - 60% without elevating portfolio default risk (PD).

Bank Portfolio Strategy: Cross-Clientele Refinancing

Industry banks holding legacy debt across studio networks, production houses, and media tech platforms can execute a synthetic recapitalization program across their client bases.

BANK CROSS-CLIENTELE REFINANCING PIPELINE

Client A: Production House: IP Rights - Underutilized

Client B: Post/VFX Studio: Data Logs - Unmonetized

Client C: Tech/Distributor: Distribution - Siloed

Bank Unified Re-Underwriting Engine —> **Single Asset Refinanced Portfolio**

- Lower WACC
- Higher LTV Collateral Base
- Tranches Issued as ABS Securities

Execution Methodology

Portfolio Asset Audit & Data Capture: Identify clients with legacy media libraries and evaluate unmonetized telemetry logs, vocal/visual performance assets, and scene metadata.

Unified Asset Re-Underwriting: Consolidate IP rights and raw dataset holdings into a single legal holding entity or pass-through structure per borrower.

Refinancing Legacy Debt: Replace fragmented, high-cost PE mezzanine debt and single-title bank loans with a low-cost, senior-secured revolving credit facility backed by the combined asset estate.

Securitization Pipeline: Package the refinanced loan portfolio into institutional Asset-Backed Securities (ABS), issuing senior tranches to investment-grade buyers and retaining servicing fees.

Capital Metric	Legacy PE/Debt Structure	Bank Refinanced (Unified Asset)	Variance / Impact
Collateral Basis	Static IP Library	IP + Live AI Training Dataset	+40% - 85% Collateral Value
Effective Cost of Debt	10.5% - 14.5%	5.5% - 7.5%	-500 to -700 bps
Borrowing Capacity (LTV)	30% of DCF	60% of DCF + Data DCF	Up to $2.5 times Debt Capacity
Asset Horizon	5-Year Forced Exit	Perpetual Cash-Flow Engine	Continuous compounding
Governance Structure	Sponsor Controlled	Borrower / Creator Co-Owned	Retains equity sovereignty

Emerging Capital Framework: The MEIT Architecture

While standard corporate holding companies can utilize unified refinancing, the Media Entertainment Investment Trust (MEIT) offers the structural framework for institutional scale.

Structure of the MEIT

Structured similarly to Real Estate Investment Trusts (REITs), the MEIT operates as a tax-efficient, bankruptcy-remote vehicle that aggregates unified IP and dataset assets.

MEIT CAPITAL & ASSET ARCHITECTURE

Institutional Capital & Creative Talent —> MEIT formation —> **Active IP Slates** (Production Yield) —> **Evergreen Catalogs** (Residual Cashflow) —> **Private Datasets** (AI Telemetry Yield)

- **Bankruptcy Remoteness**: Isolates underlying assets from single-project operational failures or production company bankruptcies.

- **Tax-Pass-Through Efficiency**: Eliminates double taxation on catalog royalties and data licensing distribution yields, maximizing debt service coverage ratios (DSCR).

- **Multi-Asset Cross-Collateralization**: Bundles active production slates, evergreen catalogs, and private dataset telemetry into a singular borrowing base.

Banking Refinancing via MEIT Conversion

Commercial banks act as the primary catalyst in this structure by funding the transition of private media entities into MEIT-compliant structures:

$$\text{DSCR}_{\text{MEIT}} = \frac{\text{NOI}_{\text{Catalog}} + \text{NOI}_{\text{Data}} + \text{NOI}_{\text{Slates}}}{\text{Principal Payment} + \text{Interest Payment}} \geq 1.65\times$$

Because the DSCR of a unified MEIT is significantly higher than that of an isolated film library, banks can issue larger senior loan syndications with tighter credit spreads.

Data Valuation and Audit Controls

To satisfy bank risk committees, data assets within the unified entity must undergo standardized valuation protocols:

Verifiability: Telemetry must be uniquely hashed, provenance-tracked, and compliant with privacy standards.

Liquidity Assessment: Valuation models must only account for datasets with active secondary market demand (e .g., multi-year enterprise LLM training contracts or real-time spatial analytics demand).

Impairment Testing: Regular stress-testing of IP cash flow decay offset by dataset growth trends.

A Proposed Strategic Conclusion

The tradition of treating media intellectual property and private dataset telemetry as distinct financial entities is an obsolete artifact of 20th-century accounting.

For industry banks, re-underwriting these components as a single unified asset unlocks non-dilutive credit capacity, compresses capital costs for corporate borrowers, and drives market capitalization expansion across media portfolios.

By transitioning away from rigid private equity structures and adopting unified asset re-underwriting—particularly through specialized vehicles using a method of Security Token Offering (STO), like the Media Entertainment Investment Trust (MEIT)—financial institutions can establish a scalable, investment-grade credit market backed by the primary engines of the modern digital economy.

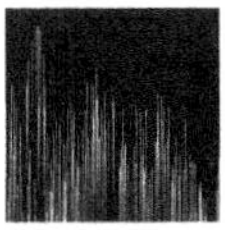

Chapter Twelve

The Executive Producer as Principal Estate Architect

The traditional role of the Executive Producer (EP) has long been that of a "*Creative Vendor*." In the legacy system, the EP is a middleman—a high-level contractor who assembles talent, secures a "Greenlight," and delivers a finished product to a studio "Landlord" in exchange for a fee. Once the delivery is complete, the vendor moves on to the next project, often with zero equity and no control over the asset's long-term financial life.

The Innovation Frontier Mandate is a fundamental redefinition of this role. It requires a total shift in identity: from a vendor who sells "content" to an **Principal Estate Architect** who governs a growing trust of wealth-generating Media IP and Private Datasets. Shifts from "selling a show" to "building a yield-bearing infrastructure."

The IP Vendor Mindset vs. The IP Manager Mindset

The difference between a creative vendor and an asset manager is the difference between a contractor and a landlord.

The Creative Vendor (Legacy): Focuses on the "Greenlight." Their primary metric of success is the production budget. They live in a cycle of "Raise, Spend, Repeat," which creates a precarious financial existence known as the "Production Treadmill." When the production ends, the income stops.

The Asset Manager (MEIT): Focuses on the Net Asset Value (NAV) and ***D-MAFFO***. They view every frame of film, every minute of a podcast, and every digital clip as a "square foot" of Media IP Property that must be managed, optimized, and leased for maximum yield.

The Industrialization of Intellectual Property

Transitioning to an Asset Manager means applying industrial rigor to the creative process. In the MEIT model, the Executive Producer ceases to be a delivery service and becomes the **Fiduciary of the Capital Stack**. *This involves three core managerial functions:*

Yield Optimization: Instead of hoping for a "backend" check that may never arrive, the Manager actively "farms" the library. This includes aggressive localization (AI-driven dubbing for emerging markets), remastering legacy assets, and cross-platform bundling.

Strategic Diversification: The Manager ensures the Trust is not over-exposed to a single genre, platform, or territory. They balance "High-Alpha" speculative projects with "Steady-State" cash flow assets (feature films, shows, limited series, YouTube channels, podcasts, and evergreen catalogs).

Risk Hedging: By maintaining an optimal Loan-to-Value (LTV) ratio and utilizing the Portfolio Shield, the Manager protects the 90% Distribution Mandate even during market volatility.

The Manager as a Fiduciary to Talent

One of the most profound shifts in this mandate is the relationship with creators. In the old model, the producer and the talent often had conflicting interests (the "Hollywood Accounting" friction).

In a MEIT, the Asset Manager acts as a Fiduciary. Because the talent holds Security Tokens (STOs), their interests are perfectly aligned with the Manager's.

When the Manager increases the Trust's ***D-MAFFO***, the talent's quarterly dividend increases.

This transparency ends the "*Creative vs. Executive*" war and replaces it with a unified mission to grow the Trust's value.

The Stake in the Ground

The Principal Estate Architect of the future is not chasing for a 'Greenlight'; they are the Governor of a Diversified IP and Data Estate. By mastering the MEIT model, you move from the 'Production Treadmill' to the Asset Grid. You are no longer just telling stories; you are architecting a sustainable, high-density utility where Media IP and Private Datasets serve as the permanent foundation for an institutional economy.

The IP Manager Mindset: Trading the "Greenlight" for NAV Optimization

In the legacy entertainment economy, the "Greenlight" is the ultimate drug. For a traditional Executive Producer, *the Greenlight represents survival*—it is the moment a studio or network agrees to fund a project, triggering production fees and keeping the lights on for another cycle. This is the Production Treadmill: a relentless, circular race where the producer must constantly sell new ideas to pay for old debts, usually surrendering 100% of the asset's long-term value in the process.

The IP Manager Mindset breaks this cycle by shifting the metric of success from the Budget to the ***Net Asset Value (NAV)****.*

The Production Treadmill vs. The Asset High-Rise

The "Greenlight" is a transaction; NAV Optimization is an evolution. When an Asset Manager looks at a piece of IP, they don't ask, "How much can I get to make this?" They ask, "How much is this worth as a permanent entry on my balance sheet?"

The Treadmill (Legacy): Success is defined by "Getting the Show Made." The producer is a creative tenant, paying "rent" to the studio in the form of lost equity. Once the show wraps, the producer's value drops to zero until the next Greenlight.

The High-Rise (MEIT): Success is defined by "Growing the Trust." Every project is a new floor added to a permanent skyscraper. Even when production ends, the "building" (the Portfolio) continues to generate D-MAFFO rent from its inhabitants (Audiences and AI Models).

Defining NAV in the Media Context

In real estate, NAV is the total value of the land and buildings minus liabilities. In a MEIT, **the Asset Manager calculates NAV by aggregating the "Future Yield" of the Bundled IP**:

Media NAV: The discounted cash flow of all future licensing, streaming, and royalty payments.

Dataset NAV: The industrial value of the Private Datasets (metadata, persona signatures, and structural stems) for AI training and synthetic media.

The Optimization Lever: The Manager increases NAV not by spending more, but by enhancing the utility of the data—through better tagging, localization, and cross-platform integration.

Strategic "Development" of the Portfolio

Trading the Treadmill for NAV optimization requires the Manager to actively "develop" the library. This is the difference between a contractor who builds a house and a landlord who manages a complex.

Eliminating the "Desperation Discount": Because the MEIT is funded by 18-Month Tranches rather than project-by-project begging, the Manager can wait for the optimal market window. They never have to sell their best "Land" (IP) just to meet payroll.

Repurposing "Scrap" into "Scale": In legacy production, "behind-the-scenes" footage and character bibles are discarded. To the Asset Manager, these are the high-margin raw materials for the Private Dataset.

Compound Licensing: A "Greenlight" producer sells rights once. An Asset Manager "leases" rights many times—segmenting the IP by territory, language, and "machine-usage" rights to maximize the density of the yield.

The Transition: From Budgeting to Allocation Chart

Feature	**The Greenlight Mindset (Producer)**	**The NAV Mindset (Asset Manager)**
Primary Goal	Secure the production budget.	Increase the value of the Trust.
View of Talent	A cost to be managed.	A partner in **Talent Equity**.
Time Horizon	Short-term (The "Delivery").	Long-term (The "Hold").
Success Metric	"The Show is Out."	***D-MAFFO*** is up.

The Stake in the Ground

NAV Optimization is a path to permanent sovereignty. By trading the 'Production Treadmill' for the 'Asset High-Rise,' the Executive Producer stops being a creative vendor and becomes a Governor of Culture. We don't just want to make the work; we want to own the Industrial Value of the work forever.

Institutional Asset Oversight: Executing the Mandatory Management Protocols to Optimize Estate Yield

In the traditional investment world, a passive fund manager simply sits back and collects dividends. However, the MEIT, structured as a Business Development Company (BDC), operates under a different mandate. By law, a BDC must make available "Significant Managerial Assistance" to its portfolio companies.

For the Executive Producer, this is not just a regulatory hurdle; it is the legal foundation for their new role. It transforms "Producing" from a creative service into a fiduciary obligation to actively "manage," refine, and harvest the value of the Media IP and Private Datasets.

The BDC Mandate: From Passive to Proactive

A BDC is designed to be an engine of growth, not a static vault. To maintain its status, the MEIT Asset Manager must demonstrate that they are providing more than just capital. They are providing the Industrial Strategy that increases the utility of the assets.

The Creative Oversight: Ensuring that new productions (The 18-Month Tranches) adhere to the high-fidelity standards required for Private Dataset licensing.

Operational Integration: Linking separate IP assets into a unified "Cultural Grid" to create cross-collateralized value.

Capital Allocation: Deciding which "Evergreen" assets require a MCAPEX injection (remastering/dubbing) to unlock new global "Rent" (Licensing Fees).

"Farming" the Library: The Manager's Daily Operations

In the MEIT Playbook, we replace the term "Production Management" with "Yield Management." The Asset Manager fulfills their BDC requirement through three specific optimization levers:

Localization and Global Arbitrage: Using AI-driven tools to dub and localize existing library assets for emerging markets (e.g., Tollywood or Southeast Asia) where the "Cost of Reach" is low but the "Volume of Data" is high.

The "Data Clean Room" Protocol: Actively managing the Private Datasets by scrubbing metadata, tagging behavioral telemetry, and preparing Persona Signatures for industrial AI training licenses.

Format Transcoding: Moving assets from legacy formats into the "Infrastructure of the Future"—preparing 4K/8K, VR-ready environments, and interactive stems that increase the Net Asset Value (NAV) for tech-sector tenants.

The Managerial Yield (D-MAFFO)

The BDC structure ensures that the Manager's "architecture" is directly tied to the performance of the token holders' yield.

The Fiduciary Filter: Every decision to "manage" an asset must pass the D-MAFFO test: Will this expenditure (MCAPEX) result in a greater increase in the ICTI (Taxable Income) or the Dataset NAV?

Transparency as Utility: Because the Manager is a fiduciary, their actions are audited. This provides Qualified Institutional Buyers (QIBs) with the confidence that the "Digital Landlord" is actively maintaining the "High-Rise" (The Dataset) rather than letting it fall into decay.

The Transition: From "Wrapped" to "Working"

Legacy Status (Passive)

- IP sits in a library waiting for a licensing call.
- The Producer's job ends at "Delivery."
- Data is "Exhaust" left for platforms to steal.

BDC/MEIT Status (Active)

- IP is actively tagged and optimized for AI training.
- The Manager's job begins at "Onboarding."
- Data is "Inventory" to be refined and leased.

The Stake in the Ground

Significant Managerial Assistance is the legal bridge between art and industry. In a BDC-structured MEIT, the Executive Producer is no longer an outsider looking in; they are the Principal Estate Architect. By actively 'farming' the library, we fulfill our legal mandate and our financial promise: to never let a single frame of film or byte of data sit idle.

The Principal Estate Architect: Managing the "Freshness" of Private Datasets through 18-Month Cycles

In the MEIT Asset Management Playbook, the Executive Producer takes on their most critical modern role: the Data Architect. Unlike physical real estate, which sits static, a Private Dataset is a living organism. If it is not constantly refreshed with new, high-fidelity human inputs, it suffers from Data Decay—a loss of industrial value as AI models seek more current and culturally relevant "training fuel."

To maintain a premium Net Asset Value (NAV), the Architect manages the portfolio through disciplined 18-Month Tranche Cycles.

The Problem: Data Decay and the "Recursive Collapse"

AI models trained exclusively on synthetic (machine-generated) data eventually suffer from "Model Collapse," where the output becomes distorted and low-quality.

The Scarcity Premium: Industrial AI clients (LLM developers, synthetic media firms) are willing to pay a massive premium for Clean, Human-Authored Data.

The Decay Factor: A dataset based on 10-year-old Media IP loses its predictive value for modern behavioral telemetry. To stay "High-Fidelity," the dataset must be continuously fed with the "Phenotype" (New Media IP).

The 18-Month Tranche: The "IP and Datasets Rotation" of Culture

The Data Architect treats production not as a one-off event, but as a Refinement Cycle. Every 18 months, the MEIT initiates a new "Tranche" of capital deployment.

Cultivation (Months 1–6): Capital is deployed into new Media IP (Films, Series, VR Experiences). This is the "Soil" preparation.

The Human Input (Months 7–12): During production and release, we capture Primary Source Data—real human reactions, dialogue nuances, and structural bibles.

Extraction & Refinement (Months 13–18): The Media IP's "exhaust" is converted into Private Datasets. This fresh data is then bundled with the legacy library, raising the overall NAV.

The Yield Event: The refreshed dataset is licensed to AI "Tenants," and the resulting GDI (Gross Data Inflow) funds the next 18-month cycle.

Managing the "Freshness Score"

The Architect uses the Tranche Cycle to maintain a high "Freshness Score" for the portfolio. This ensures that the 144A Rail investors are not buying a decaying asset, but a self-renewing utility.

Legacy Assets (The Base): Provide historical context and stylistic consistency.

Fresh Tranche Assets (The Delta): Provide current linguistic patterns, modern visual aesthetics, and up-to-date behavioral telemetry.

Feature	**Legacy Library (Static)**	**18-Month Tranche (Dynamic)**
Data Type	Historical/Reference	Predictive/Behavioral
Industrial Use	Style Transfer/Consistency	Core Model Training
NAV Impact	Stabilizes Floor	Drives Growth (Alpha)
Architect's Goal	Preservation	**Freshness Injection**

Preventing Synthetic Dilution

The Data Architect's primary mandate is to ensure that the Private Dataset remains 100% Human-Authored.

The Audit: Every 18 months, the dataset undergoes a Proof of Human Authorship (PoHA) audit.

The Protection: By refreshing the data with genuine human creativity, the MEIT creates a "Moat" that machine-only studios cannot cross. The more the world is flooded with "cheap" AI content, the more the MEIT's "Fresh" human data appreciates in value.

The Stake in the Ground

> Data is not a static commodity; it is a perishable crop. The Data Architect understands that to keep the 'Oil' flowing, you must keep the 'Soil' fertile. By managing the 18-Month Tranche Cycle, the Executive Producer ensures the MEIT never suffers from decay. We aren't just making movies; we are generating the Fresh Human Intelligence that the digital world needs to transact with.

The Principal Estate Architect serves as the Governor of a Diversified IP and Data Estate

Moving beyond the constraints of traditional project-based approvals to *manage a high-density utility.* By mastering the MEIT model, you transition from the "Production Treadmill" to the **Asset Grid**, shifting your focus from isolated creative transactions to the oversight of a permanent, yield-bearing infrastructure. You are no longer just telling stories; you are architecting a sustainable, market-driven ecosystem where Media IP and Private Datasets serve as the foundational bedrock for institutional wealth and competitive markets.

By adopting this institutional role, you transition from a "*Creative Vendor*" to the primary authority of your own financial ecosystem. You utilize the ***D-MAFFO*** metric and **ICTI** baseline to verify the reality of your yield, turning pixels and performance into "**Digital Land/Buildings**" that is liquid, protected, and bankable. This is the evolution of media leadership—where the architect doesn't just build the house, but owns the grid, ensuring that culture remains a protected asset class for long-term capital appreciation.

Chapter Thirteen

The Producer's Syndicate: Global MEIT Formation

The transition from a solo producer to a Global MEIT Syndicate is the move from "*making a movie*" to "**founding a cultural IP and data grid.**" For example, when a core group of 5 to 8 executive producers aligns, they cease to be competitors for studio overhead and instead become the General Partners (GPs) of a diversified, multi-national asset class.

The Aggregation Protocol: Consolidating the "Land/Buildings"

The first stage for a group of 5 to 8 producers is the Consolidation of Shadow Value. Each producer brings a "siloed" catalog of legacy IP and a future pipeline. The Syndicate's first task is to strip away the legacy noise and audit the collective Information data pooled.

The Audit of Title: The group performs a unified legal sweep to identify "Clean" IP—assets where they hold the primary right to harvest Private Datasets.

The Bundle Strategy: Instead of 8 small portfolios, the Syndicate creates "Thematic Bundles" (e.g., a "Global Noir" bundle or a "Sci-Fi Infrastructure" bundle). This creates the Institutional Density required to attract Qualified Institutional Buyers (QIBs) on the 144A Rail.

The Shared SPV: Each producer's contribution is mapped to a specific compartment within a "Master MEIT" structure, ensuring individual protection while benefiting from the group's collective Net Asset Value (NAV).

Cross-Border Distribution: The Global Yield Arbitrage

A syndicate of 8 producers is naturally multi-national. This geographic diversity is the "**Secret Sauce**" of the Global MEIT, allowing the group to exploit Yield Arbitrage across different regulatory and consumer markets.

Territorial Optimization: The Syndicate identifies which regions provide the best M-Yield (Consumer Rent) versus which regions provide the highest-fidelity Private Datasets for AI training (e.g., capturing unique linguistic nuances in emerging markets).

The Stablecoin Settlement: By utilizing a Stablecoin for all internal and external distributions, the Syndicate works with the friction of international banking. A producer in Seoul and a producer in London receive their 90% Pass-Through simultaneously, in the same currency, at the same second.

Global Regulatory Masking: The group utilizes the 144A Rail to navigate complex international securities laws, offering a single, unified "Smart Security" to global institutions rather than 8 separate regional offerings.

The Governance Council: Managing the 18-Month Tranche

The final component is the transition from "*Creative Control*" to **Fiduciary Governance**. The 5 to 8 producers form the Investment Committee of the MEIT, managing the industrial cadence of the portfolio.

Tranche Allocation: The Council meets to decide how capital is deployed across the 18-month cycle. They move from "project-based" thinking to "Asset-Management" thinking—balancing high-risk/high-reward "Hits" with stable, high-margin Private Dataset harvests.

The Veto of Origin: The Council acts as the final arbiter of Proof of Human Authorship (PoHA). They ensure that no "synthetic rot" enters the vault, protecting the premium valuation of the collective Sovereign Signature.

The Exit Strategy: Because the equity is tokenized, members of the Syndicate can achieve "Partial Liquidity" by selling portions of their tokens on the secondary ATS (Alternative Trading System) without needing to dismantle the entire production house.

Syndicate Formation Matrix Chart

Phase	Action	Outcome
I. Aggregation	8 Libraries → 1 Master Vault	**Institutional Density / NAV Floor**
II. Arbitrage	Global Pipeline → Global Rails	**Stablecoin Yield / Cross-Border Liquidity**
III. Governance	8 Producers → 1 Investment Committee	**Industrial Cadence / Asset Protection**

The Stake in the Ground

A single producer is a freelancer; a Syndicate of eight is an Institution. By forming a Global MEIT, we move beyond the 'Scarcity Mindset' of the studio system and into the 'Abundance Mindset' of the Executive Coalition. We are no longer asking for permission to produce; we are providing the global market with the Asset-Backed Infrastructure it craves. Together, we don't just tell stories—we own the Grid they run on.

Chapter Fourteen

The Agency & Management Evolution

For a century, the '*Hollywood Model*' has been built on a fundamental conflict of interest: the agent or manager prioritizes the largest upfront check to secure a commission, while the creator requires long-term sustainability. This misalignment often leads to '*career burning*'—**the extraction of short-term cash flow at the expense of the talent's long-term valuations and equity in their intellectual property.**

The MEIT replaces this extractive relationship with the **Fiduciary Alignment Model**. By utilizing Tokenized Equity, the manager moves from being a "*collector of fees*" to a "**partner in growth**."

From Commissions to "Carried Interest"

In the Sovereign Issuance framework, the manager's compensation is no longer a "*tax*" on the creator's labor. **Instead, it is structured as Carried Interest within the Trust.**

The Old Way: The manager takes 10% of a $1M fee. If the project loses money or the creator's brand is damaged by the role, the manager still keeps the $100k.

The MEIT Way: The manager receives a percentage of the Security Tokens (STOs) issued for the 18-Month Tranche. Their wealth is now mathematically tethered to the Net Asset Value (NAV) and the ***D-MAFFO*** yield of the client's entire Digital Portfolio.

The Result: The manager only thrives if the asset thrives. They are incentivized to protect the Persona Signature from overexposure or low-value licensing.

The Multi-Family Office (MFO) Structure

As agencies evolve into **Asset Aggregators**, they begin to function as Multi-Family Offices (MFOs) for the creative class. This goes beyond "*booking jobs*" and enters the **realm of institutional wealth management**.

Treasury Management: The manager oversees the client's Stablecoin inflows, ensuring the 90% distribution is reinvested or diversified according to the client's long-term goals.

Asset Protection: The manager acts as the "Gatekeeper of the Vault," ensuring that no third party can access the Private Dataset without a high-margin, Sovereign-compliant contract.

Succession Planning: Because the equity is tokenized and held within a Sovereign Estate, the manager helps the client build a "Legacy Vault" that continues to pay out to heirs and foundations automatically through smart contracts.

Ending the "Churn" – The Retention Advantage

The "Hollywood Model" is notorious for talent jumping from agency to agency. Tokenized equity creates a "Trusted" Fiduciary Bond.

Vesting Schedules: Management tokens can be subject to vesting periods tied to the 18-Month Tranche cycles. This ensures the manager stays focused on the long-term health of the Private Dataset.

Co-Investment: For the first time, managers can "buy into" the tranches alongside their clients, putting their own capital at risk to show absolute conviction in the Aggregation Strategy.

Alignment Matrix: Commission vs. Fiduciary Equity Chart

Feature	Legacy "Hollywood" Model	The Fiduciary MEIT Model
Primary Incentive	Volume of Deals	Growth of NAV / Yield
Risk Profile	Zero Risk to Manager	Shared Downside (Principal Risk)
Client Relationship	Transactional / Contractual	Equity Partnership (Tokenized)
Long-Term Focus	Next 3–6 Months	The 100-Year Estate

The Stake in the Ground

We are evolving beyond the extractive 'Middleman' model and establishing the 'Fiduciary Partner' as the new standard. By aligning incentives through Tokenized Equity, we ensure that the manager's success is a direct reflection of the talent's equity holdings. Our goal is to move past the simple 'deal-closer' and empower Asset Architects—visionaries capable of building a Cultural IP and Data Grid designed to sustain and generate value for generations.

From Commissions to AUM: How Agencies Transition into Asset Aggregators

In the legacy entertainment model, the agency is a "*transactional*" service provider. Their revenue is tied to the Commission—a 10% slice of a one-time contract. This model is inherently fragile, relying on the constant churn of new deals to survive. **In the MEIT ecosystem**, *the agency undergoes a fundamental evolution*, to including a new revenue stream of an **Asset Management business**.

By shifting their focus from "*Deals*" to **AUM** (Assets Under Management), agencies transition from being "middlemen" to being the Institutional Aggregators of the Diversified IP and Data Estate.

The Evolution of the 10% Commission

The traditional commission model fails in the AI era because it cannot capture the long-tail value of a Media IP and Private Dataset.

The Problem: An agency might negotiate a $1M acting fee for a film, taking $100k. But if that film's data (the "Skyscraper") generates $10M in AI-licensing yield over the next decade, the legacy agency has no structural claim to that value.

The Shift: Agencies move toward a Management Fee + Performance Carry model. They stop "selling" talent and start "managing" the talent's Private Dataset Vault.

The Agency as a "Land/Building Assembler"

In the MEIT framework, the agency's primary role is Aggregation. They act as the "*Zoning Authority*" that prepares the talent's IP and data for the 144A Rail.

Data Curation: The agency no longer just books auditions; they oversee the "Harvesting" of the 18-Month Tranche. They ensure the client's Persona Signature is high-fidelity and legally "Clean."

Portfolio Construction: Agencies bundle their clients into Thematic MEITs (e.g., a "Comedy Powerhouse" bundle or a "Global Language" bundle).

Fiduciary Responsibility: The agent evolves into a Financial Advisor, helping the talent convert their "Profit Points" into Security Tokens that provide lifetime liquidity.

The AUM Model: Building the Endowment

By moving to an AUM model, the agency builds a "**Permanent Endowment**" for its clients. Instead of a series of one-off checks, the agency manages a diversified portfolio of Bundled Assets.

The Management Fee: A percentage of the ***D-MAFFO*** generated by the client's vault, providing the agency with steady, "Rent-like" income.

The Carry: A performance-based incentive tied to the growth of the Net Asset Value (NAV) of the MEIT.

Asset Stickiness: In the commission model, a client can leave and the income stops. In the AUM model, the agency and client are "Co-Owners" of the SPV, creating long-term structural alignment.

Structural Comparison: *Talent Agency vs. Asset Aggregator Chart*

Feature	Legacy Talent Agency	MEIT Asset Aggregator
Revenue Model	10% Transactional Commission	**2% Management / 20% Carry (AUM)**
Asset Focus	The Next Gig (Services)	**The Private Dataset (Property)**
Time Horizon	Short-term (Quarterly)	**Generational (The 18-Month Cycle)**
Client Relation	Representation	**Fiduciary Partner / Co-Investor**

The Stake in the Ground

The era of the 'Agent as a Salesman' is over. We are entering the era of the 'Agent as an Architect.' By transitioning from commissions to AUM, agencies are finally able to capture the true industrial value of their clients' brilliance. We aren't just booking jobs anymore; we are managing Diversified IP and Data Estates that grow in value while the world is entertained.

The Principal Estate Manager: Governing the Client's Digital Portfolio and Persona Signatures

In the legacy era, a representative's job was to manage a person—their schedule, their auditions, and their public image. In the MEIT era, the "**Principal Estate Manager**" manages a Digital Portfolio. They move from being a scheduler to a Portfolio Manager, treating the talent's "***Persona Signature***" with the same fiduciary care a wealth manager treats a diversified stock and bond portfolio.

This shift ensures that the creator's Identity is not a depreciating marketing tool, but an appreciating Sovereign Asset.

The Persona Signature: The Private DNA

The Persona Signature is the unique, high-fidelity metadata that defines a creator's professional essence. It is the "Digital DNA" harvested during the 18-Month Tranche.

Linguistic & Behavioral Stems: The specific cadence, tone, and vocabulary that make a performance unique.

Visual Geometry: The 3D/Volumetric data and motion-capture signatures that allow for ethical synthetic expansion.

The Ethical Boundary: The Representative ensures that this signature is only licensed under "Restricted Use" contracts, preventing the "Deepfake Dilution" of the client's brand.

Managing the "Bundled IP and Dataset Portfolio"

The Principal Estate Manager Representative categorizes the client's output into three distinct "*Risk/Yield*" buckets within the Private Dataset Vault:

The Active Layer (The Performance): Managing the current "Human-in-the-loop" contracts—films, series, and live appearances. This generates the immediate M-Yield.

The Infrastructure Layer (The Stems): Managing the library of raw assets (dialogue, outtakes, bibles) that feed the GDI (Gross Data Inflow) through AI training licenses.

The Legacy Layer (The Perpetuity): Managing the "Evergreen" rights that ensure the client's Private Persona continues to generate yield for their estate, long after their active retirement.

The "Zoning" of the Persona

Just as a real estate manager zones land for commercial or residential use, the Principal Estate Manager Representative

"Zones" the client's Persona Signature for specific industrial utilities:

Commercial Zone: High-value, high-visibility licensing for global brand campaigns.

Industrial Zone: Deep-learning licenses for LLMs or internal studio toolsets.

Public Zone: Restricted, fan-engagement layers for the Sovereign Community (Reg A+ holders).

Task	Legacy Representative	Sovereign Representative
Asset Type	Time & Labor	**Persona Signature (Data)**
Legal Focus	Work-for-Hire Contracts	**Sovereign Title & Provenance**
Technology	Email / Phone	**The Private Dataset Vault**
Value Protection	Public Relations (PR)	**Encryption & Proof of Human Authorship**

The Fiduciary Handshake: PoHA and Provenance

The Representative's most critical new duty is the **Audit of Origin**. They must certify that every asset in the portfolio carries the **Proof of Human Authorship (PoHA)**.

By maintaining a "Clean" chain of provenance on the Private Ledger, the Representative guarantees that the client's data commands a **Premium Valuation**. They protect the "*Signature*" from being polluted by unauthorized synthetic replicas, ensuring that when the market wants the real talent, ***they must pay the Trust's Floor Price***.

The Stake in the Ground

> We are moving from 'Booking Agents' to 'Asset and Identity Architects.' The Principal Estate Manager Representative doesn't just look for the next job; they build a Digital Fortress around the client's career. By managing the Persona Signature as a high-density asset, we ensure that the creator's influence is no longer a fleeting moment, but a Permanent Infrastructure of the global cultural grid.

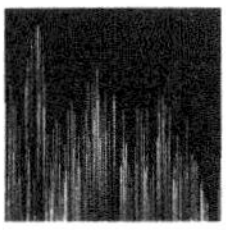

Chapter Fifteen

Why Family Offices and Top Talent Might Unite to Build 21st-Century Studios

The traditional Hollywood studio system was built for a different century. *Its foundation relied on massive physical lots, centralized distribution pipelines, and opaque accounting practices*. Within that system, two critical groups were routinely kept at arm's length from true ownership: the family offices supplying patient capital and the elite creators driving the culture.

Family offices seeking exposure to media were typically funneled into high-risk slate financing or passive, single-project equity checks. Talent—the writers, directors, showrunners, and performers—operated on isolated islands, competing for project-by-project backend participation that rarely yielded long-term wealth.

That legacy architecture is no longer fit for purpose.

As streaming economics compress and data, AI, and digital networks redefine how media value is generated, a fundamental shift is underway. The construction of 21st-century global studios relies on direct, unmediated collaboration between patient family capital and top-tier creative talent.

The Alignment Gap in Legacy Media

Historically, both family offices and creative talent suffered from the same structural vulnerability: unhedged exposure in a single-deal environment.

For Family Offices: Investing in media meant placing speculative bets on individual Special Purpose Vehicles (SPVs) with binary outcomes—high downside risk, minimal governance, and zero participation in underlying data or catalog yields.

For Creative Talent: Artists were treated as transactional fee-takers. A hit show or blockbuster film enriched the studio balance sheet, but left the creator without a permanent equity stake in the ecosystem they created.

When capital and craft are separated by layers of 3rd party overhead, neither side achieves long-term wealth preservation. 21st-century studios resolve this mismatch by eliminating middleman frictions and aligning patient capital directly with primary creative engines.

Why the Traditional Private Equity Model Fails Media & Creators

When institutional investors attempt to disrupt traditional studio models, their default playbook is often the standard Private Equity (PE) buy-and-build strategy. However, applying classic PE playbooks to creative enterprises creates severe structural friction for both patient capital and top talent:

1. The Mismatch of Timelines vs. IP Perpetuity

PE funds operate on rigid 3-to-7-year investment horizons dictated by internal rate of return (IRR) targets and forced exit cycles. But high-quality intellectual property, evergreen catalogs, and private datasets do not decay on a corporate schedule—they are perpetual revenue engines. Their value compounds over decades as franchises expand, distribution windows reset, and emerging technologies (like generative AI models) create new licensing demand for legacy assets. Forced PE liquidations sever this multi-generational yield just as it begins to compound.

2. Short-Term Stripping vs. Long-Term Data Yield

Standard PE models rely heavily on leverage, debt loading, and aggressive cost-cutting to maximize immediate EBITDA for a fast resale. In modern media, this approach guts the creative infrastructure and ignores the underlying asset: the continuous generation of scene telemetry, audience analytics, and computational data. A PE model treats content as a consumable product to be flipped, rather than a permanent, yield-generating data estate.

3. Talent Alienation & Governance Friction

In a traditional PE rollup, talent is squeezed into strict financial governance where sponsors retain total control over IP decisions and exit timing. Creators become short-term employee-contractors tied to earnouts rather than true equity partners in an enduring estate, alienating the very visionaries required to build the studio's perpetual asset base.

> To build a modern studio, family offices and creators need a structural mechanism built around long-term asset retention, perpetual data monetization, and shared equity sovereignty—not forced PE exit clocks.

The Plural Estate: The MEIT Engine

Inspired by the capital efficiency and institutional stability of Real Estate Investment Trusts (REITs), the Media Entertainment Investment Trust (MEIT) establishes a bankruptcy-remote, multi-channel asset framework.

Instead of funding isolated movies or forced-exit PE portfolios, family offices and top talent co-invest as true equity partners in a plural asset estate. This structure bundles three core asset classes into a unified engine:

Active Production Slates: Diversified IP properties developed across multiple genres and global formats.

Evergreen Catalog Rights: Income-generating library titles that yield steady, long-tail residual streams.

Private Datasets & Scene Telemetry: High-margin secondary yield generated through advertising content, audience telemetry, spatial metadata, and clean-room AI model licensing.

Why Family Offices Require Direct Talent Alignment

Family offices manage multi-generational capital. Their mandates prioritize wealth preservation, inflation-hedged income, transparent governance, and compounding equity—metrics that legacy entertainment accounting and rigid PE funds fail to deliver consistently.

By co-founding 21st-century studios alongside top creative talent through a MEIT, family offices secure:

Portfolio Risk Management: Transitioning from volatile single-title bets into cross-collateralized, risk-adjusted media estates.

Direct Ownership: Holding transparent, first-lien equity alongside the primary visionaries who control the intellectual property.

Monetizable Data Revenue: Capturing the expanding value of private scene telemetry and computational rights as media content becomes essential training input for global AI frameworks.

Why Creators Are Partnering with Patient Capital

For world-class storytellers, bypassing legacy studios and PE financial sponsors to partner directly with private capital represents the ultimate step toward complete creative and financial autonomy.

From Contractors to Co-Founders: Talent moves from chasing short-term greenlight checks or PE earnouts to holding real, compounding equity in an expanding media estate.

Insulated Creative Freedom: The predictable, recurring income generated by the trust's underlying catalog and dataset assets insulates creative decisions from short-term market panic, protecting artistic integrity.

Private Data Protection: Creators ensure their visual, vocal, and performance telemetry is ethically managed, properly licensed, and continuously monetized to their direct benefit.

Building the Next Generation of Global Studios

The 21st-century studio will not be defined by soundstage acreage, legacy television networks, or short-term PE rollups. It will be built as a lean, *capital-efficient*, data-sovereign asset engine powered by direct partnership between family office capital and visionary storytellers.

By applying the structural clarity of the MEIT framework to talent-capital partnerships, family offices and creative leaders are doing far more than financing content—*they are co-building permanent,* **generational media estates designed for long-term yield.**

Appendix: The D-MAFFO Financial Framework

Note: while the individual components of the equation are rooted in established financial and tax law, the specific synthesis of the D-MAFFO equation—and its application to the MEIT dual-asset class of Media Entertainment IP and Private Datasets—is an original, one-of-a-kind financial vehicle.

The "North Star" of the MEIT

While traditional media conglomerates obscure performance behind the "black box" of EBITDA or "Net Income"—metrics often distorted by the complexities of "Hollywood Accounting"—**the MEIT operates** on the ***D-MAFFO*** (Distributable Media-Adjusted Funds From Operations) framework.

***This is a proprietary evolution of the traditional* Real Estate Investment Trust (REIT) metric, FFO.** It has been specifically recalibrated to account for the unique lifecycle of Intellectual Property (IP) and the high-margin utility of Private Datasets. It is designed to reveal the true cash velocity of a media portfolio by stripping away non-cash accounting artifacts and accounting for the specific recurring obligations of the cultural grid.

The ***D-MAFFO*** is the core financial engine of the MEIT. It strips away non-cash accounting "noise" and applies a mechanical volatility buffer to ensure a sustainable, asset-backed yield.

In the MEIT framework, Investment Company Taxable Income (ICTI) serves as the rigorous, audited bedrock upon which the ***D-MAFFO*** metric is constructed. While legacy media accounting often relies on subjective "net profit" definitions, this dual-layer approach aligns media finance with the transparency standards of institutional real estate and regulated investment funds.

The D-MAFFO Equation:

$$\textbf{\textit{D-MAFFO}} = [\textbf{ICTI} + (\textbf{D\&A}) - (\textbf{C}_{\textbf{E}})] \textbf{ X } (\textbf{1} - \textbf{Delta R}_{\textbf{P}})$$

components:

ICTI (Investment Company Taxable Income): This is the audited net income of the Trust. It already accounts for gross revenues ($\mathbf{R_L + R_D}$) and has subtracted operational expenses, management fees, and interest ($\mathbf{O_E + A_M + I_D}$). By starting with ICTI, the MEIT eliminates "creative accounting" and ensures the 90% distribution mandate is the floor.

D&A (Depreciation & Amortization): These are non-cash charges that reduce ICTI for tax purposes but do not leave the bank account. Adding these back reveals the actual liquid cash capacity of the library.

C_E (Capital Expenditures): This represents the cash spent on recurring maintenance of the library (e.g., remastering, security updates for datasets) that may not be fully captured in the ICTI operating expenses.

1 - Delta R_P (The Mechanical Adjustment): The multiplicative risk buffer that discounts the cash flow based on the portfolio's specific exposure to concentration risk, regulatory shifts, or technological decay.

Component Breakdown:

R_L (Licensing Revenue): Gross receipts from media IP distribution and sub-licensing.

R_D (Data Revenue): Gross income from private dataset utility leases and AI training licenses.

O_E (Operating Expenses): All direct costs associated with asset maintenance and digital distribution.

A_M (Asset Management): Fees for the strategic oversight and optimization of the Trust.

I_D (Interest/Debt Service): Costs associated with leverage used to acquire the asset library.

D&A (Depreciation & Amortization): The add-back of non-cash amortization of creative intangibles to reflect actual cash yield.

Delta R_P (Delta Risk Premium): The mechanical adjustment for portfolio-specific risk.

ICTI: The Audited Bedrock

ICTI is a tax-compliant figure calculated according to specific regulatory standards (such as those governing Business Development Companies or Real Estate Investment Trusts).

Function: It represents the "clean" taxable income of the Trust before the deduction of dividends paid to shareholders.

The 90% Mandate: Because a MEIT is designed as a pass-through utility, it must distribute at least 90% of its ICTI to maintain its tax-advantaged status.

Role in the Equation: ICTI provides the verified baseline that prevents the "leakage" of value typically seen in opaque production contracts.

Why ICTI is the "Clean" Baseline

In the ***D-MAFFO*** equation, using ICTI instead of GAAP "Net Income" provides a superior institutional anchor:

Eliminates Corporate Noise: ICTI focuses on the earnings of the investments (the Media/Data licenses) rather than the parent company's general overhead.

Regulatory Certainty: Because ICTI is a tax-reported figure, it is harder to manipulate than internal "Net Profit" calculations. It provides a "Hard Floor" for the 90% Mandate.

Cross-Border Compatibility: For global investors, seeing the yield calculated from a recognized tax baseline (ICTI) provides the comfort of Sovereign Transparency.

D-MAFFO: The Operational Velocity Metric

While ICTI satisfies the tax man, ***D-MAFFO*** (Distributable Media-Adjusted Funds From Operations) satisfies the investor. It adjusts the ICTI to reflect the actual operational cash flow generated by the Dual-Core assets (Media Entertainment IP and Private Datasets).

The Relationship: Why Both Matter

The relationship between ICTI and ***D-MAFFO*** is what creates Institutional Grade Certainty:

Transparency: ICTI ensures the Trust isn't hiding money in "overhead" or executive bonuses.

Valuation: *D-MAFFO* provides the "Multiple" used to determine the Net Asset Value (NAV). When an institutional buyer looks at a MEIT, they aren't looking at "star power"; they are looking at the stability of the D-MAFFO yield relative to the ICTI baseline.

The "Liveness" of the Estate: Because ICTI is reported to regulators and ***D-MAFFO*** is reported to the market (often via the Security Token rail), the "Gap" between the two tells the story of the library's health.

In short: ICTI proves the income is real; *D-MAFFO* proves the income is sustainable.

Why D-MAFFO is Unique

The originality of the equation lies in three specific "Structural Innovations" that do not exist in legacy media or standard Real Estate Investment Trusts:

The Hybrid Asset Baseline (ICTI + GDI)

Traditional metrics (like FFO) only measure one type of "rent." ***D-MAFFO*** is the first equation to baseline Investment Company Taxable Income (ICTI) by aggregating two distinct revenue streams into a single industrial flow:

Consumer Rent (M-Yield) multiplied by the Industrial AI Leases (GDI)

The Amortization "Add-Back" for Digital Skyscrapers

In standard accounting, media assets are treated as "depreciating equipment" (like a truck that wears out). ***D-MAFFO*** treats Media IP as "**Digital Land**" and the resulting metadata as a "**Skyscraper.**" By adding back **$Amort_{IP}$** , the equation recognizes that the Private Dataset actually increases in utility as AI models evolve, even as the "IP" ages.

The Mechanical Volatility Buffer (Delta RP)

Standard financial formulas are static; they show what happened in the past. The inclusion of the **Risk Premium Delta** (**Delta R_P**) makes ***D-MAFFO*** a dynamic governor. It is the only equation in the media space that mechanically adjusts "*Available Yield*" based on real-world platform and territorial instability, creating a self-fortifying Portfolio Shield.

The Competitive Advantage: A "Financial Utility" Chart

Feature	Legacy "Net Profit"	Standard REIT FFO	Sovereign D-MAFFO
Transparency	Opaque / Discretionary	Transparent / Institutional	**Immutable / On-Chain**
Tax Structure	Corporate Double-Tax	90% Pass-Through	**90% Pass-Through (BDC)**
Risk Handling	Subjective Write-downs	Market Fluctuations	**Mechanical $\Delta RP Buffer**
Asset Class	One-off Projects	Physical Buildings	**Bundled IP + Private Data**

The Stake in the Ground

The ***D-MAFFO*** equation is the **Proprietary Benchmark** of your financial architecture. It is a singular innovation because it ends the era of 'Creative Guessing' and replaces it with **Audited Industrial Certainty**. It transforms the traditional studio model into a **Financial Utility**, providing the only standardized formula in existence that accurately values human authorship and private datasets within a market-driven, institutional framework.

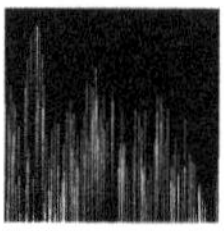

Appendix: 10-Year MEIT Capital Allocation Simulation

To understand the long-term viability of the MEIT model, we must analyze the tension between Physical Dilution (issuing more tokens) and Economic Accretion (increasing the value and yield per token).

In a traditional startup, *dilution is often viewed as a "loss" of control*. However, in a REIT-style **MEIT**, periodic equity raises are the primary engine for scaling the "building." If the Asset Manager ensures that every raise is Accretive, the early equity holders end up with a smaller percentage of a significantly larger, more stable, and higher-yielding cash-flow machine.

The 10-Year MEIT Growth Projection

This simulation assumes a 10-year horizon with an 18-month raise cycle (the "Heartbeat"), totaling six major capital events. The goal is to transition the portfolio from a "Seed Portfolio" to an "Institutional Grade Library."

Analysis of the "First Equity Holder" Position

The Power of ***D-MAFFO*** per Token:

Early talent, founders, and seed investors will see their ownership percentage decrease over time. However, because the MEIT is a yield-driven vehicle, the metric that matters is ***D-MAFFO*** per Token.

Year 1: You own 10% of a $10M portfolio yielding $1M (Your share: $100k).

Year 10: You own 2% of a $500M portfolio yielding $50M (Your share: $1M).

The Result: *Even though you were "diluted" from 10% to 2%, your annual dividend income increased 10x.*

Secondary Market Appreciation:

Unlike a private production company where equity is frozen, the STO model allows early holders to benefit from Multiple Expansion. As the MEIT de-risks, institutional appetite increases:

Early Stage: Tokens may trade at 5 times ***D-MAFFO***.

Mature Stage: Tokens trade at 12 times ***D-MAFFO*** (aligning with blue-chip REITs).

Competitive Edge: Mitigating "Bad Dilution"

To protect early equity holders, the MEIT Playbook employs three specific financial safeguards:

The Accretion Hurdle: The Smart Contract or Board only approves a new raise if the projected D-MAFFO per Token increases post-raise. If a new acquisition doesn't increase the dividend for existing holders, the raise is blocked.

Anti-Dilution Warrants for Talent: A-list talent can be granted "Performance Warrants" that trigger new token issuances if the portfolio hits specific NAV milestones.

The Debt-First Buffer: By using Revolving Credit Facilities (Debt) to fund smaller productions between raise cycles, the MEIT delays equity issuance until market conditions are optimal.

The Simulation: $15M Seed Case Study

Starting with a $15M Seed moves the MEIT out of the "Venture" risk profile and into the "Institutional" profile instantly. It provides the "Critical Mass" needed for Master Lease leverage.

Core Assumptions:

Initial AUM: $15,000,000 (Evergreen Asset Base).

Seed Investment: $100,000 (0.66% initial ownership).

D-MAFFO Margin: Constant 10% of total AUM.

Dividend Payout: 90% of D-MAFFO (The Pass-Through Mandate).

10-Year Capital Allocation Table Simulation

Year	Portfolio AUM	Total D-MAFFO	90% Dist. (Total)	Seed Ownership %	Seed Annual Div.
Year 1	$15,000,000	$1,500,000	$1,350,000	0.66%	**$8,910**
Year 3	$45,000,000	$4,500,000	$4,050,000	0.45%	**$18,225**
Year 5	$120,000,000	$12,000,000	$10,800,000	0.32%	**$34,560**
Year 7	$350,000,000	$35,000,000	$31,500,000	0.24%	**$75,600**
Year 10	**$1,000,000,000**	**$100,000,000**	**$90,000,000**	**0.16%**	**$144,000**

Note: In the final $1B phase, the seed investor's original $100k stake generates $144,000 in passive income annually—a 144% cash-on-cash yield, even after significant dilution.

Strategic Insights: The $15M "Proof of Power"

Reduced Terminal Dilution: Starting larger means you issue less equity in later rounds. Your final ownership remains higher (0.16%) compared to a $5M start.

The Efficiency Frontier: Fixed costs (Audits, KYC/AML, Security) are static. At $15M, overhead drops to ~5% of income, compared to ~15% for a $5M fund.

Immediate Master Lease Leverage: A $15M library represents 2-3 major Evergreen catalogs. You don't ask for "test deals"; you dictate Master Lease terms from Day 1.

Dilution vs. Accretion Logic (The "Economic Magic")

The most critical check is the relationship between AUM Growth and Ownership Dilution.

The AUM Growth: The portfolio grows 66.6x (from $15M to $1B).

The Dilution: The seed investor is diluted by only 4.1x (from $0.66% to $0.16%).

The "Asset Manager" Summary

Over a decade, the first equity holders transition from Speculators in a Project to Shareholders in a Media Utility.

Years 1–3 (The Risk Phase): Reliance on key assets; dividends may vary as the library is optimized.

Years 4–7 (The Scaling Phase): The 18-month cycles build the "Wall of Content." Cross-collateralization stabilizes the yield.

Years 8–10 (The Institutional Phase): The MEIT is now a Price-Maker. It dictates terms to streamers, and early holders enjoy a high-yield, liquid asset that functions like Digital Real Estate.

The Stake in the Ground

> The MEIT architecture solves the dilution paradox: by executing 18-month raise cycles at progressively higher Net Asset Values (NAV), we ensure that Economic Accretion consistently outpaces Physical Dilution. We aren't just issuing more tokens; we are increasing the 'Density of Yield' per shard, ensuring that early stakeholders own a smaller percentage of a vastly more valuable and productive industrial engine.

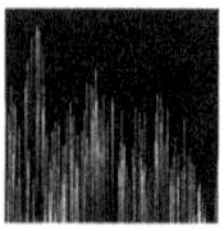

Appendix: Talent Equity Participation Summary - The MEIT Advantage

This example summary is designed to be presented to high-level talent (or their agents/lawyers) to demonstrate why **equity in a MEIT** (Media Entertainment Investment Trust) is fundamentally superior to traditional "back-end points."

It reframes their contribution from a "work-for-hire" participation into a Foundational Partnership in a liquid, cash-flowing asset class.

Talent Equity Participation Summary: The MEIT Advantage

Prepared for: [Talent Name / Production Entity]

Asset Management Firm: [Your MEIT Name]

1. Executive Intent: Real Equity vs. Paper Points

Traditional "Back-end Participation" is often subject to "Hollywood Accounting," where overhead, cross-collateralization, and creative interest charges ensure that "Net Profits" rarely materialize.

Under the MEIT Asset Management model, you are granted Security Tokens (STOs) that represent a direct ownership stake in the entire Trust's library. You aren't just hoping for a "hit"; you are participating in the Institutional Yield of a diversified IP portfolio.

2. Why This Model Wins for A-List Talent

A. Immediate & Continuous Yield (The 90% Rule)

Because the MEIT is structured as a pass-through entity, it is legally mandated to distribute 90% of its taxable income to shareholders.

The Benefit: Instead of waiting years for a "profit" check, you receive quarterly distributions based on the MAFFO (Media-Adjusted Funds From Operations) of the entire library. This is the "rent" collected from global streamers, paid directly to your digital wallet.

B. Transparency & The Smart Contract Waterfall

The days of auditing a studio's books are over. Your equity is managed via a Smart Contract Waterfall.

The Benefit: When a licensing fee is paid by a platform like Netflix or Amazon, the code automatically splits the revenue. Your share is calculated and distributed instantly, bypassing the studio's "internal accounting" delays.

C. Secondary Market Liquidity

Traditional equity is "locked" until a company is sold or an IPO occurs.

The Benefit: Your STO tokens can be traded on regulated digital exchanges after a standard vesting period. If you need liquidity, you can sell a portion of your stake on the secondary market without waiting a decade for a studio buyout.

3. Portfolio Synergy: You Own the "Building," Not Just the "Room"

As an equity stakeholder in the MEIT, your tokens represent a cross-section of all assets under management.

Diversified Risk: If your specific project is in a "dry season" between licensing windows, your dividends are sustained by the WALT (Weighted Average Lease Term) of the Trust's evergreen assets and social channels.

The Accretion Effect: Every time the MEIT uses an 18-Month Raise Cycle to acquire new high-performing IP, your tokens become Accretive. The growth of the Trust's market cap increases the value of your existing shares without you having to lift a finger on a new set.

4. Comparative Summary: Legacy vs. MEIT

Feature	Legacy Studio "Back-end"	MEIT STO Equity
Accounting Basis	"Net Profits" (Highly Subjective)	**MAFFO (Cash-Flow Centric)**
Payout Frequency	Rare / Multi-year delays	**Quarterly (90% Pass-Through)**
Audit Requirement	Necessary & Expensive	**On-Chain / Real-Time Audit**
Liquidity	Zero (Until buyout/exit)	**High (Secondary Digital Exchanges)**
Asset Scope	Single Project	**Total Diversified Portfolio**

5. The "Stakeholder" Commitment

By accepting MEIT Equity, you are recognized as a Creative Founder. You are incentivized to help the Trust scale, as every increase in the Net Asset Value (NAV) of the library directly correlates to the value of your tokens.

In the MEIT model, *the talent becomes the landlord of the culture they create.*

Appendix: Risk & Mitigation

Engineering the Institutional Shield

In the legacy entertainment world, risk is a "bug" that producers hope to avoid through luck. **In the MEIT framework**, risk is a "variable" that we neutralize through structural engineering. To move the needle from a $15M seed to a $1B institutional utility, we must address the "Big Four" risks that keep traditional investors on the sidelines.

The Volatility Risk (The "Flop" Factor)

The Risk: A high-budget production underperforms, cratering the Trust's quarterly earnings and causing a sell-off of tokens.

The MEIT Mitigation: The 80/20 Rule: We mandate that 80% of the AUM is anchored in Evergreen (cash-flowing) assets. Only 20% is ever exposed to the "High-Alpha" speculative sleeve.

Cross-Collateralization: The D-MAFFO generated by the library's "Digital Land" covers the debt service of the new projects, ensuring the 90% dividend remains sacred regardless of a single film's performance.

The Tenant Concentration Risk (The "Streamer Squeeze")

The Risk: A major Anchor Tenant (e.g., Netflix) chooses not to renew a Master Lease, or attempts to "low-ball" the renewal rate.

The MEIT Mitigation:

The Exit Option & Optionality: Because the library is diversified, the Asset Manager has "Hold Power." We can move the bundle to a rival platform, transition to a high-yield AVOD (Ad-supported) model, or fragment the rights across global territories.

WALT Management: By staggering the Weighted Average Lease Terms across the portfolio, we ensure that no more than 15% of the Trust's revenue is up for renewal in any single 6-month window.

The Technological Risk (The "Smart Contract Failure")

The Risk: A vulnerability in the Smart Contract Waterfall leads to a loss of funds or a breach in the Compliance Layer.

The MEIT Mitigation:

The Multi-Sig Firewall: The Digital Treasury is governed by a 3-of-5 multi-signature protocol requiring approval from the Asset Manager, a third-party auditor, and an independent compliance officer.

Immutable Security Audits: Every line of code in the STO Engine undergoes a "Triple-Audit" by top-tier blockchain security firms before a capital tranche is opened.

The Regulatory Risk (The "SEC Shift")

The Risk: Global regulators change the rules regarding Security Tokens or Private Datasets, threatening the Trust's legal standing.

The MEIT Mitigation:

The Programmable Compliance Layer: Our tokens (ERC-1404/SRC-20) are "Regulation-Aware." We code KYC/AML and jurisdictional logic directly into the asset. If a law changes, the smart contract is updated globally to reflect the new restriction, ensuring the Trust is "Compliant by Design."

The BDC Shield: By operating under the Business Development Company (BDC) or REIT-style framework, we utilize 60+ years of established case law rather than operating in a "gray market" crypto space.

Risk vs. Mitigation: *The Matrix Chart*

Risk Category	Legacy Status	MEIT Mitigation Strategy
Accounting	Opaque "Net Profit"	**Audited D-MAFFO Transparency**
Liquidity	5–10 Year Lock-up	**24/7 Secondary Market (ATS)**
Production	Binary (Hit/Miss)	**Portfolio Cross-Collateralization**
Compliance	Manual / Reactive	**On-Chain / Proactive Logic**

The Stake in the Ground

Risk in a MEIT is not avoided; it is managed through math. By replacing the 'Hollywood Black Box' with a transparent, automated, and diversified Institutional Shield, we transform the inherent volatility of culture into the industrial stability of real estate. We don't bet on the weather; we own the umbrella.

Glossary

This glossary defines the financial and technical pillars of the MEIT framework.

Core Financial Metrics:

D-MAFFO (Media-Adjusted Funds From Operations): The primary yield metric for the MEIT. Unlike "Net Profits," D-MAFFO is an audited, real-time calculation of cash flow generated by IP and data, after accounting for maintenance and debt service, but before non-cash depreciation.

NAV (Net Asset Value): The total market value of the Trust's underlying IP Media and Private Datasets, minus liabilities. This is the "Floor" used to price new token tranches during the 18-Month Heartbeat.

Accretive Raise: A capital event where new tokens are issued at a price higher than the current NAV, ensuring that the yield per token increases for existing holders despite physical dilution.

WALT (Weighted Average Lease Term): A metric borrowed from commercial real estate measuring the average remaining time on all active Master Leases in the portfolio. A higher WALT indicates higher income stability.

Structural Architecture:

Master Portfolio Lease: An institutional-grade contract where a streamer or AI developer leases an entire "bundle" of IP or data for a fixed term, replacing individual "work-for-hire" project contracts.

Anchor Tenant: A global platform (e.g., Netflix, Anthropic, Disney+) that provides the "Base-Load" revenue for the Trust through long-term, high-volume licensing agreements.

The 18-Month Heartbeat: The rhythmic cycle of the MEIT, involving a 6-month acquisition phase, a 6-month optimization phase, and a 6-month valuation/re-raise phase.

Cross-Collateralization (Institutional): The process of using the surplus yield from "Evergreen" assets to provide a financial backstop for new, high-alpha productions, effectively "hit-proofing" the dividend.

Digital & Data Strategy:

The Content Loop: A retention strategy that integrates high-frequency vertical content (Shorts, TikToks, etc) with feature-length IP to eliminate "Ghost Town" periods and reduce subscriber churn.

Algorithmic Synergy: The use of owned digital channels to drive external search volume and "direct-link" traffic, forcing a streamer's internal algorithm to prioritize the MEIT's assets.

Private Datasets: Proprietary, non-public data collections (viewership patterns, metadata, creative libraries) leased to

AI developers for model training under a sovereign issuance model.

The Data Bridge: A mandatory lease condition requiring the tenant (streamer) to provide real-time API access to engagement metrics, allowing the Asset Manager to audit the "Rent" and NAV accurately.

Technological Foundation:

STO Engine (Security Token Offering): The regulated software layer that fractionalizes the MEIT's equity into liquid, tradable shards.

Smart Contract Waterfall: The programmable logic that automatically executes the distribution of licensing fees: allocating for taxes, maintenance, and the mandatory 90% pass-through to token holders.

Programmable Compliance: "Regulation-Aware" code embedded in the token that automatically enforces KYC/AML and jurisdictional restrictions, making the asset "Compliant by Design."

Digital Land/Buildings: The conceptual shift of viewing IP and Private Datasets as productive acreage/square feet that generates "Rent" rather than "Sales."

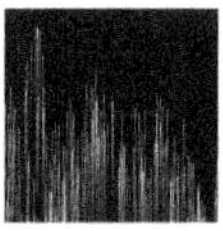

About the Author

Matthew Ashburn is a visionary strategist operating at the high-stakes intersection of entertainment finance and digital asset architecture. ***As the principal architect of the MEIT*** (Media Entertainment Investment Trust) framework, Ashburn has pioneered a structural revolution that empowers creators, executive producers, and agencies to act as the ultimate fiduciaries of their own cultural asset class.

His work focuses on the strategic securitization of intellectual property portfolios, specifically through the innovation of bundling fragmented licensing revenues into high-velocity, professional-grade portfolios. By integrating the Security Token Offering (STO) framework, Ashburn is proposing a solution to a historical problem of media illiquidity, *creating a Liquidity Stack that allows for the 24/7 securitization and trading of media assets under regulated protocols.*

Ashburn's methodology is dedicated to removing the volatility from art and the opacity from legacy accounting. The book provides a potential roadmap for the modern media leader to transition from a project-to-project cycle into a media entertainment IP and private datasets powerhouse model—where culture is the collateral, transparency is the standard, and yield is the law.

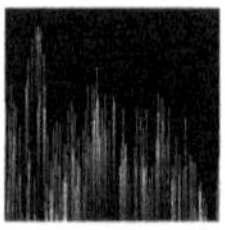

About: A&D Playbook Series

The **Assets & Data Playbook Series** is a foundational collection of strategic manuals designed to bridge the gap between creative influence and institutional finance. In an era where legacy systems are fracturing, this series provides a playbook with a focus on "Digital Assets & Private Datasets"—the modern leader who understands that the future of wealth is built on the securitization of intellectual property and the optimization of global licensing data.

The series serves as a technical and strategic roadmap for navigating the transition from transactional business models to asset-backed portfolios. Each installment focuses on removing the volatility inherent in creative industries by applying rigorous financial engineering, regulatory compliance, and digital-asset innovation.

By centering on the **MEIT (Media Entertainment Investment Trust)** framework, the series establishes a new standard where culture is treated as collateral, and transparency is the primary driver of value and equity.

This series is engineered for:

Executive Producers seeking to self-fund through securitized yield.

Talent Agencies and Management Companies transitioning to AUM-based revenue streams.

Family Offices looking for a legacy, defensive, non-correlated asset class.

Digital Asset Architects building the next generation of regulated asset-backed STOs.

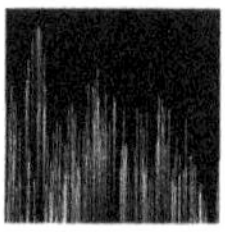

The MEIT Playbook
delivers a groundbreaking thesis on rebuilding the studio from the asset-backed class up.

Authored by principal architect Matthew Ashburn, this guide adapts REIT mechanics and Security Token Offerings (STOs) to cross-collateralize creative IP with high-margin AI data licensing streams. By moving away from speculative single-project deals,

the Media Entertainment Investment Trust (MEIT) establishes plural, asset-backed portfolio structures that re-underwrite content and datasets as Digital Land and Buildings.

The Assets & Data Playbook Series

ISBN 979-8-9929021-8-1
52999
9 798992 902181